D1161623

FRESH-
WATER
FISHING

FRESH-WATER FISHING

Trevor Housby

Galley Press

First published in Great Britain in 1983 by
Blandford Press

This edition published in 1988 by
Gallery Press
in association with Octopus Books Limited
59 Grosvenor Street
London W1

Copyright © 1983 Blandford Books Ltd

All rights reserved. No part of this book may
be reproduced or transmitted in any form or by
any means, electronic or mechnical, including
photocopying, recording or any information
storage and retrieval system, without permission
in writing from the Publisher.

ISBN 0 86136 630 1

Printed in Czechoslovakia
50677

Contents

Introduction 7

Barbel 9

Bream 16

Carp 33

Crucian Carp 47

Chub 53

Dace 60

Eels 67

Grayling 74

Perch 78

Pike 87

Roach 109

Rudd 120

Tench 126

Trout 134

Sea Trout 144

Zander 147

Index 149

To Russel James Housby,
Hopefully an Angler

Introduction

Although I am a keen all-round angler and have fished in most parts of the world, freshwater fishing remains one of my favourite pastimes. Nowadays that term, 'freshwater fishing', encompasses not only coarse fishing but trout fishing as well. During the past decade still-water trout-fisheries have become established throughout the British Isles, bringing fly fishing within the range of most anglers. For the relatively cheap price of a day permit, the freshwater angler can now fly cast for brown, rainbow, brook or hybrid trout: fish which were once out of reach of the average angler. Add to this the multitude of first-class day-ticket and club-controlled coarse-fishing waters and it is obvious that today's freshwater anglers have ample opportunity to fish to their hearts content.

Freshwater anglers are lucky enough to have a wide variety of freshwater species to fish for, and fishermen who wish to specialise in one particular type of fish can usually find a productive water within travelling range of their homes or can plan a holiday expedition to an area where they know these fish can be located. Specialised fishing is extremely popular and in England anglers from all over the country travel down to Christchurch in Dorset to fish for the giant barbel that live in the River Avon, while pike enthusiasts, on the other hand, head north to the lochs of Scotland in hope of hooking one of the monster pike known to exist in these vast waters.

This travelling, in search of a certain fish, is part of the fascination of freshwater fishing. I remember making one long-range and difficult trip from Hampshire to the Lake District to catch char. These fish seldom top 16 oz (0.45 kg) in weight but their beauty and rarity make them a much sought-after species. On this particular trip the weather was vile and snow, high winds and icy roads made the water difficult to reach, but the fish were in a feeding mood and I brought home a reasonable catch of beautiful char ... I could go on to describe other successful (and unsuccessful) sorties of this kind, all of which have increased my love of freshwater fishing.

The signs are that our fishing can only get better. Awareness of pollution, the constant striving of water authorities to improve the rivers, restocking programmes; all are combining to paint a rosy picture for future generations of anglers. Twenty years ago things were not so good but now the message is loud and clear. Water is life, pollute it and you kill not only fish but many other forms of life. Today's angler has the opportunity to fish good waters. Tomorrow's angler should and with luck will have an even greater chance of sport.

Barbel

The barbel is a member of the carp family but unlike the true carp which prefers slow moving or still water the barbel is a fish of the faster rivers. In shape the barbel is a long, cylindrical fish and with its large and powerful fins and strong tail it is well adapted to life in heavy currents. The eyes are rather small and are set high up and far back on the head. Barbel take their name from the four *barbels* (appendages) they possess, two on the tip of the snout and two at the corners of the lower lip. The lower jaw is completely underslung and this, coupled with the four barbels which act as feelers, help the fish to root for food in the mud and gravel of the river bed.

Spawning occurs in late April or early May when the mature fish seek out shallow water; the eggs then hatch out in 12 to 15 days. Unfortunately, little is known about the movement of very young barbel, and it is rare for a barbel under 9 or 10 in (23–25 cm) to be taken on rod and line.

The barbel record is held jointly by three specimens, each weighing 14 lb 6 oz (6.52 kg), two from the Hampshire Avon and one from the Thames.

Barbel are found only in a few rivers in England. So far as I know they are not present in any Scottish, Irish or Welsh rivers. In the South of England the main barbel waters are the Thames and two of its tributaries, the Kennet and the Lea. The Thames and Kennet still hold good heads of these fish, some of which grow to prodigious size, while the Lea barbel tend to be rather small in comparison. The Hampshire Avon and the Dorset Stour are good waters also containing some very large barbel. Yorkshire has a number of barbel rivers, namely the Ouse, Nidd, Wharfe, Ure, Swale and Derwent. Barbel are now common in the River Severn where they provide consistent sport for both the pleasure and the match angler alike. Limited numbers of barbel are found in other waters, notably the Bedfordshire Ouse and the River Wensum in Norfolk.

Feeding habits

Barbel are almost entirely bottom feeding fish taking much of their nourishment from weeds and underwater plants. In the early part of the season they will often chase and eat small fish but as the season advances they return to browsing along weed-beds and underwater ridges.

Baits

Most of the popular baits including bread baits, worms, min-nows, maggots, cheese, meat, grain and seed will tempt barbel, but on some rivers the fish show a marked preference for certain foodstuffs. Avon barbel show an addiction for meat-based baits – cubes of tinned luncheon meat being their favourite – though at one time they were taken in numbers on cheese cubes or on cheese paste and both baits are still worth using. Barbel also show a distinct liking for hempseed and many Thames barbel are taken on this bait. However, hempseed is banned on many rivers and before using it an angler should check local regulations carefully. Meat-based baits are in my opinion the best all-round barbel baits. Even sausage can be used to good effect. Whenever I fish for Lower Thames barbel I buy 1 lb (0.45 kg) of pork or beef chipolatas and use them raw. The best way to use an uncooked sausage is to snip off both ends and hook it through once (see Fig. 1). This enables the barbel to pick up the bait and suck out the inside, thereby whetting its appetite to take the remainder of the sausage into its mouth.

Groundbaits

Barbel respond well to groundbaiting and I have found that the groundbait should always consist of the same substance and be of an equal size as the hook bait. For example, if lobworms are the chosen bait then the groundbait should be whole lob-worms. If meat is used then the groundbait should be meat, and so on.

10

(Fig. 1)

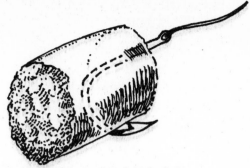

Uncooked sausage makes a good bait for barbel

Tackle

Rods

Barbel are powerful fish which require relatively heavy tackle. There are now custom-built barbel rods available. These are constructed from both fibreglass and carbon fibre. For all-round barbel fishing two rods are essential, one for float fishing, one for legering. The ideal rod for float work is a 12 ft (3.6 m) trotting rod. This has an all-through action ideal for picking line off the water on the strike. While a 10 or 11 ft (3-3.3 m) carp rod is ideal for legering, this rod is capable of casting big baits on heavy leads and for handling heavy fish in fast weedy waters.

Reels

Either a free-running centre-pin or a fixed-spool reel will be needed, depending on the style of fishing to be adopted.

Lines

Barbel are immensely strong, consequently it is wise to use a line of at least 6 lb (2.7 kg) breaking strain. If possible and if you can afford it then it is always wise to buy the best line available. Test the last two or three yards of it after each outing. If any weakness shows, the weak part should be cut away until the line shows its original strength. Many anglers don't bother to do this and then complain when a sizeable fish breaks free. Nylon has a lot of elasticity, so when striking at a fish from a long way off the rod needs to be pulled right back over the shoulder before the hook will drive home.

Hooks

Normally a size 4 or 6 will be sufficient but as barbel prefer a big bait I never use anything smaller than a size 8, except when using maggot or hempseed. Then I use a size 12, 14, or 16 hook depending on the size of bait being used. Barbel seem to frequent the more snagged-up areas of a river and when fishing for barbel a number of hooks are often lost on various underwater obstructions. I use good quality eyed hooks, in particular the Sundridge specimen hooks. Many expert barbel anglers prefer to use spade-end hooks. The French *Lion D'Or* being the favourite pattern.

Floats

As barbel tend to be shy, the size of float should be kept down to the minimum weight that the water and the strength of current require.

Leads

For fast, heavy water the type of weight known as an Arlesey bomb is the most successful. A good supply of various sizes should always be carried as this will avoid wasting a whole day's fishing because the leads available are of the wrong weight for the water.

Methods (early season)

Float fishing

A shallow fast swim should be chosen for barbel-hunting in the early part of the season, as the fish will still be in the swift water recovering from spawning. Weir pools especially produce large numbers of early-season fish and the most pleasant method of taking barbel under these conditions is with float tackle.

The angler needs to station himself at the head of the chosen swim. Groundbait must then be introduced into the water: slowly and in moderation at first, gradually building up until a constant stream of food is being washed through the swim. It is often rewarding to do nothing but groundbait for the first hour so that the barbel get used to the food and accept it without fear. Then the tackle, suitably baited, should be swung out a little upstream of the chosen pitch, making sure that if the bed of the river is clear the bait just rolls down across it. If the swim has a number of snags the float must be set so that the hook bait trails a few inches above the bottom.

As a rule barbel bites are decisive and bold, pulling the float straight down and out of sight. It is easy to connect with this kind of bite, provided the angler keeps a cool head.

Despite their preference for fast water, barbel, particularly the extra-large fish, will sometimes feed in slack water on the edge of a current. Under these circumstances it is possible to take a fish by laying on in the slack water (see Fig. 2). This technique has accounted for many huge barbel, some topping 12 lb (5.4 kg) in weight.

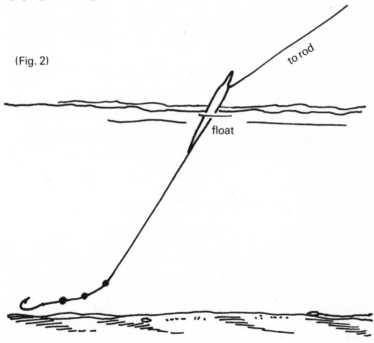

(Fig. 2)

float

to rod

Laying on in slack water

Barbel dislike being confined in keep nets and should, in my opinion, be returned immediately to the water. For obvious reasons they should be released upstream of the swim that is being fished. It is essential to become acquainted with every corner of a barbel swim and you would be well advised to begin operations close to the bank, gradually increasing the distance of the cast until every possible barbel-lie has been covered.

Legering

In a shallow swim the weight of the lead should be just a little too light to remain still in one place. Its slow and hesitant roll downstream will ensure that the whole swim is carefully covered. On hard-fished waters where most of the fish have been hooked and returned a swim feeder or block-end feeder can be used to good effect. This type of bait dropper seems to work best for me when the barbel steadfastly refuse to move out from under the trailing weed fronds. The trick is to roll the feeder in to where the barbel are. Bites often follow immediately. In some cases fair bites are registered due to the larger barbel actually picking up the entire block-end feeder rather than the bait. Barbel that consider themselves to be in a safe position often become easy to hook. Find a barbel swim that has never been fished and results can be spectacular.

(mid season)

As the season progresses, barbel tend to move out of the shallows into deeper water while still keeping to swims that have a constant flow of heavy water running through them. Late summer barbel often become largely nocturnal in habit and although it is still possible to catch fish during the daytime, the serious barbel angler will do well to confine himself to evening or night fishing. Of course, on some waters night fishing is illegal, but where it can be practised it will, over a period of time, yield a better-than-average catch.

At night, float fishing is obviously out of the question and the angler has, therefore, to fall back upon the use of leger tackle which creates the obvious difficulty of detecting bites. Many anglers hold their rod all the time and although this enables even the slightest pull to be clearly felt, it can become extremely tiring, even with a lightweight outfit. I myself favour propping the rod up on one rest so that the tip is clearly defined against the night sky, for I find it seldom becomes so dark that the tip of the rod cannot be clearly seen. I know a great many anglers who use a torch of the cycle-lamp variety, lying on its back under the rod. I am against the use of lights when night fishing, for I feel that even a faint glimmer of diffused light coming from a normally dark portion of the river bank tends to make the barbel, already a very wary fish, even more cautious.

The way in which a barbel's bites are registered when legering is something of a mystery – for no two fish give an identical pull. For instance, I have known one barbel make the rod tip slightly vibrate, while the next cast has produced a pull which practically jerked the rod out of the rest. These varied bites make the timing of the strike a question on which no two barbel anglers ever agree. I strike at the slightest movement and so far have been quite successful. Perhaps next season I shall have to change my ideas completely for barbel are strangely unpredictable creatures.

If night fishing is not allowed on the chosen water then fish during the hours of dawn or dusk using either float or leger, whichever is felt to be the most suitable method for the occasion.

Until recently barbel fishing was thought to be a summer occupation and was confined completely to the warmer months. It has now been shown that barbel feed quite well during the winter and good sport can be had, even on a raw day. Of course, during the colder weather fish move back and stay in the really deep water instead of moving about as they do in summer. If a deep hole can be found close to the bank on a known barbel water it will usually hold fish and can be fished with either float or leger tackle.

Bream

Anglers for bream often talk of their catches in terms of stones of even hundredweights of fish. Because of this, bream have a reputation for being stupid in that they can be caught one after the other. To some extent this is true, for when a big shoal of hungry bream is located it is quite possible to catch fish after fish in quick succession. These huge shoals usually consist of fish of between 2 and 4 lb (0.9–1.8 kg) in weight. Really large bream are a very different proposition; not only are they extremely cautious, they also only feed in very small shoals, so that it is almost impossible to catch large quantities of specimen bream at one sitting.

Bream are found in rivers, canals, lakes, reservoirs and lochs throughout Britain and Ireland. Often the largest specimens are taken from large but shallow lakes. The Cheshire meres are a prime example of the type of water most likely to produce specimen bream.

There are two types of bream in Great Britain. These are the common or bronze bream which is widely distributed, and the silver bream. This latter fish, which has a very limited distribution and a very low weight, is of little interest to most anglers. The common or bronze bream, however, is an extremely popular fish. Its wide distribution and its comparatively high average size are undoubtedly the main reasons for its popularity; for being common to most areas it is within reach of many anglers. By general standards, bream of 3 or 4 lb (1.4 or 1.8 kg) are average fish, a 5 pounder (2.3 kg) is a good one and any bream over 6 lb (2.7 kg) is a specimen. Although the bream record stands at 13 lb 8 oz (6.12 kg), very few anglers ever manage to catch a bream of over 7 lb (3.2 kg) in weight. During most years bream between 9 and 13 lb (4.1-5.9 kg) are reported to the angling press.

Most of the really big bream caught in this country have been taken by night anglers, fishing large still waters. Catching big bream, like most forms of specimen hunting, requires long hours of concentrated effort for very few bites. This kind of fishing does not appeal to everyone but it is necessary if specimen fish are to be caught consistently – and bream are no exception to this rule. Big bream fishing is, however, becoming increasingly popular and already several new and effective techniques have been developed specifically for bream fishing. These tactics are already producing results and no doubt in future years more and more big bream will be taken.

Feeding habits

The bream is a bottom feeding fish which seldom rises to the middle or upper water levels in search of food. Consequently most anglers fish for bream on or very close to the bottom. This is particularly true of still-water bream, for in slow moving rivers anglers often catch large numbers of small bream by trotting a bait slowly downstream. The main food of these fish consists of minute aquatic insects or larvae of the many free-flying insects which start life in the water. Bloodworms are a constant source of food for bream. In waters where fresh water mussels abound these form an important part of the larger bream's food chain. Medium and large bream make a consider-able nuisance of themselves by taking the huge baits used by carp anglers, which has given bream a bad reputation with many dedicated carp anglers.

A large shoal of hungry bream can eat vast quantities of food and, because of this, bream fishermen often employ huge quantities of groundbait to attract and hold feeding bream shoals which happen to pass within casting distance of the bank.

Baits

Although bream have large appetites they can be extremely finicky in their choice of food. As bait that caught fish one outing may produce very poor results the next, it is advisable to make a point of carrying a selection of baits on all bream fishing expeditions. Worms, bread baits and maggots are all good bream catchers and probably account for more bream per season than any other baits.

Worm is probably the best all-round bait to use as, being natural, the bream tend to accept it without question. Unfortunately worms also attract other fish, which make a thorough nuisance of themselves by snapping-up worm-baited tackle long before the bream have had a chance to find it. Almost any worm can be used as bream bait but redworms or lobworms are best. Redworms can be used singly or in bunches of three or four. These bunched-worm baits are very effective where large bream are concerned. It seems likely that the bream sees the ball of wildly wriggling redworms as a mass of enlarged bloodworms and takes them accordingly. Lobworms can be used whole or can be broken in half. The tail end of a big lobworm makes a very effective bream bait. Where possible it is advisable to avoid hooking a worm bait too many times; this spoils the natural appearance of the bait. Unfortunately worms are rather soft and where long casting techniques have to be employed to reach the feeding bream shoal, it is often essential to hook the worm two or three times to ensure that it is not torn off the hook during casting.

Bread paste, flake and crust are all effective bream baits and can be used with confidence on most waters.

On a clean bottom which is devoid of blanket weed or really soft mud, bread paste is a favourite bait. Unfortunately, it is heavy in comparison with other bread baits and will quickly sink from sight into soft weed or the ooze of a mucky-bottomed swim. Flake on the other hand is ideal. Being light it will sink slowly and come to rest gently on top of the weed or mud. This is an important point to remember and it pays to find out as much as possible about the bottom of every swim you intend to fish. Breadcrust, fished on leger or float tackle, can also be used to combat the problem of bottom weed, for the crust, being naturally buoyant, will rise as far as the trace between hook and weight will allow and will remain suspended on or just above the blanket of weed.

Bream of all sizes can be caught on maggots used singly or in large bunches. Once again, small fish can make a nuisance of themselves by gorging the maggot baits before bream have a chance to get to them. Combination baits, of maggot and bread flake or paste (see Fig. 3), are good for bream.

(Fig. 3)

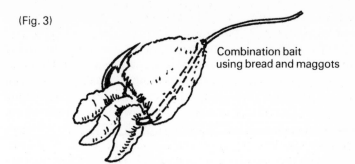

Combination bait
using bread and maggots

Another highly successful bait is tinned sweetcorn used singly or doubled up to make a larger bait (see Fig. 4). Sweetcorn needs no preparation and can be used straight from the tin. Loose grains should be thrown or catapulted into the swim as an attractant. Extra large bream can often be taken on small baits. A single maggot or a tiny worm may well produce the fish of a lifetime.

(Fig. 4)

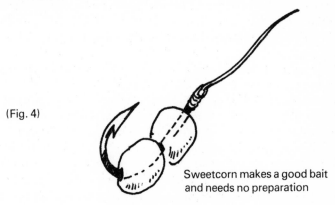

Sweetcorn makes a good bait
and needs no preparation

Groundbaits

Few specialist bream anglers use less than 30–40 lb (13.6–18.1 kg) of groundbait in a single session. Although this may sound an incredible amount of groundbait to the average angler, a shoal of bream is capable of clearing a vast amount of food in a remarkably short space of time. Once they have exhausted the food potential of a swim, they move on quickly to fresh pastures. Consequently it takes a considerable quantity of groundbait to attract the attention of a bream shoal and almost as much again to hold the fish in the swim for a whole day's fishing.

Breadcrumbs, sausage, rusk and pigmeal can all be used for groundbait. Many anglers make the mistake of adding too much water to their bream groundbait, so that it breaks up on hitting the surface of the water. This is wrong, for to be effective the groundbait should sink rapidly to the bottom in one lump and then gradually break up. In this way a thick carpet of groundbait can be laid along the bottom. Great care should be taken to throw the groundbait out fanwise so that the swim is thoroughly baited (see Fig. 5). Once attracted to a swim, bream can be held by throwing out fresh quantities of groundbait at regular intervals throughout the fishing period. By doing this correctly the bream can be held in the swim for a lengthy period.

(Fig. 5)

Groundbait should be thrown out fanwise,
so that it thoroughly baits the swim

Although heavy groundbaiting is generally an essential part of bream fishing, it can be a disadvantage where really big bream are concerned. Really big bream live and feed in very small shoals and too much groundbait can easily over-feed a shoal which may contain only six or eight fish. On waters where the bream are few and far between but of a large size it is advisable to restrict the quantity of groundbait used. Samples of the hook bait can be added to the groundbait mixture, chopped worms, maggots and lumps of bread paste all add to the attraction of basic groundbait.

Location

Fish location is a major problem for the bream angler and, unless the water in question is over-run with bream, the individual shoals can be extremely difficult to find. Although overstocked waters will produce large aggregate weights of fish and can usually be relied on to fish well under most conditions, they are unlikely to produce any worthwhile specimens. Because of this it is advisable deliberately to seek out waters that hold a limited stock of bream, for these are the ones most likely to produce bream of specimen size.

Bream are an obliging species. On a hot still evening when the water temperature is high they will give themselves away by rolling and priming on the surface. Bream anglers consider this act a prelude to feeding: whether or not this is true is difficult to say. By careful observation it is possible to get a rough idea of the size of the fish likely to be caught from a swim, as bream shoals are usually made up of fish of equal size. Consequently if fish of an estimated 3-4 lb (1.4-1.8 kg) are sighted then it is likely that the bulk of the fish caught from that swim will be of a similar size. Personal observation leads me to believe that as the fish get larger the size of the shoal decreases, until a handful of huge fish are left from a shoal which originally contained a hundred or more low to medium-weight specimens. Because of this it always pays to take a careful note of any really outsize bream seen rolling, and to fish the swim where the fish was sighted. In this way it is often possible to catch a couple of extra large specimens.

During the early weeks of the season, bream often move into shallow water to cleanse themselves after spawning. Many anglers, however, are still convinced that shallow water produces poor catches. This is a grave mistake, for it is pointless to fish a nice comfortable swim that has a good depth of water if the fish are at the other end of the water splashing about in the shallows. Later, as the season progresses the shoals will forsake the shallow water and work back into the deeper swims.

Having located a water which holds a few shoals of bream, it is a good idea to map thoroughly the water in question. Mark each swim in which bream have been caught or sighted and each weed bed, ledge, hole or snag. By doing this job properly it is possible to build up an accurate picture of the water and, more important still, of the movement of the bream shoals that it contains. A project of this kind takes days but it is time well spent and in the long run it will help solve the problem of locating bream.

Bream like carp and tench are basically a summer species. However, on rivers they can still be caught during cold weather, at times when lake fish are noticeable only by their absence.

Tackle

Bream have the reputation of being poor fighters which has led many anglers to use extremely light tackle. It is true that bream seldom make long, fast runs when hooked but, make no mistake, a big bream is more than capable of smashing comparatively heavy tackle by its sheer bulk and doggedness. The extreme depth of a bream's side makes it an awkward proposition, for once it turns and makes off parallel to the bank it can be extremely difficult to stop and turn. Many an experienced bream angler has had his tackle smashed by bream that have made off in this fashion. A big bream can put up quite an awe-inspiring battle, particularly when hooked in very deep water, and for this reason it pays to use fairly substantial tackle for all aspects of bream fishing.

Rods

To the best of my knowledge no rod manufacturer produces a rod especially for bream fishing. Most of the big bags of medium-weight fish are taken on 12 or 13 ft (3.6 or 4 m) glass or carbon match rods. The specialist angler relies more on leger tactics and is inclined to use a 10 or 11 ft (3 or 3.3 m) rod of the MKIV Avon type. There are many suitable rods available and any good tackle shop will be able to show you a range of these rods. The ideal bream rod has a test curve of approximately $1\frac{1}{4}$ lb

(0.6 kg). This will comfortably handle lines of 4–7 lb (1.8–3.2 kg) breaking strain and will be suitable for all aspects of bream fishing.

Reels

A medium sized fixed-spool reel is ideal for bream fishing. By carrying two or three spare spools, each loaded with a different strength of line, it becomes a simple enough operation to switch tackle several times as circumstances dictate during the course of a day.

Bream tend to feed well away from the bank and long casting is often essential. To enable long casts to be made with ease always make certain that your fixed-spool reel is loaded to within $\frac{1}{8}$ in (0.3 cm) of the lip of the spool.

Lines

It is inadvisable to fish with a line under 4 lb (1.8 kg) breaking strain where big bream are concerned, for the sheer bulk of the fish can break a line on the strike and as already mentioned a big bream, hooked in deep water, can apply considerable pressure. In very weedy water it is advisable to use a line of 6 or 7 lb (2.7 or 3.2 kg) breaking strain. That extra strength can make all the difference between landing or losing your fish among the weed stems or fronds.

Hooks

Size of hook depends on the size of bait and for bream fishing it is advisable to carry a range of hooks from size 4 down to size 14. The smaller hooks are used with small worm, maggot or cereal baits, while the larger hooks are used for bunches of redworms, lobworms, large lumps of bread paste or crust.

When the bream are really 'On', it is worth checking your hook point at frequent intervals. Once a hook becomes blunt it can cost you a lot of fish.

Swing tip and target

Top match anglers are continually trying to perfect a method of bite detection that will allow them to catch the maximum quantity of fish in the shortest possible time. One item of tackle developed for this purpose has proved its worth so conclusively that it deserves a place in every keen angler's tackle box. I am, of course, referring to the swing tip (see Fig. 6) which was designed specifically for detecting the gentlest of bream bites.

Although originally designed for bream fishing, the swing tip can be used equally well with roach, rudd or tench. The swing tip is simply a flexible extension to the rod, which screws on to the rod-tip ring. It carries several ordinary rod rings through which the line runs in the conventional way. When a swing tip is used, the rod should be set parallel to the bank. This is essential for bite detection. The strike can then be made parallel to the bank so that the line is pulled through the water. An upward strike causes delay, due to water pressure, and may lead to lost fish. The rod tip should only be raised when the fish is actually hooked.

Match anglers have given a great deal of thought and time to developing terminal tackle to be used in conjunction with the swing tip. Their research has proved that a certain type of 'link leger' gives the best results. This leger is made up as follows. First take a 6 or 8 in (15-20 cm) length of 7 or 8 lb (3.2 or 3.6 kg) breaking-strain nylon, tie a $\frac{3}{16}$ diameter split ring to one end and a swivelled bomb of suitable size to the other. The reel line should then be passed through the split ring, the hook being tied directly to the end of the reel line. A leger stop is then nipped on to the line and the tackle is ready for use. The distance between the stop and hook depends upon the prevailing mood of the fish. A 2 ft (60 cm) trail is the most useful, but the stop can be moved up or down the line as required. Once the tackle has been cast out, the line must be tightened so that the swing tip hangs down, forming an angle (see Fig. 6) between rod tip and leger weight. The slightest pull will then be clearly indicated by an upward movement of the tip. If the taking fish moves in towards the bank, the tip will drop downwards.

Although the swing tip was originally developed for use on slow flowing waterways it works well on still waters. Match anglers are, of course, more interested in quantity than quality, but the swing tip can also be used, most successfully, to take bream of specimen size. Swing tipping over a long period of time can be a tiring occupation as the tip must be watched at all times, otherwise bites may be missed. Constant practice is required to perfect the technique of swing tipping, but once it has been fully mastered it can be most productive.

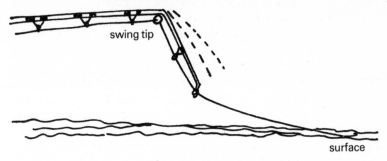

(Fig. 6) Although developed for use with bream, the swing tip is also effective when used with roach, rudd or tench

swing tip

surface

Numerous variations of the original swing tip are now available. All, however, work on the same principle.

Experts seldom agree on the question of what length of rod should be used with the swing-tip extension. Some prefer the longer rods while other, equally successful, anglers are convinced that a 9 or 10 ft (2.7 or 3 m) rod is quite adequate. It is largely a matter of personal choice what length of rod is used; though in my opinion the shorter rods are probably the best as they have a slightly stiffer action and are also much lighter.

The only practical reel to use for swing tipping is a fixed spool; centre pins being totally useless for this method of fishing. Most good tackle shops stock swing tips. They can also be made at home from long plastic knitting needles and light, small diameter polythene tube.

Butt-bite indicator

A simple bite indicator can be made by hanging a loop of silver paper over the line between the first and the second rod ring (see Fig. 7). This makes a crude but highly effective bite indicator.

There are a large number of bite indicators in common use for night fishing. These range from the simple silver-paper indicator already mentioned through to commercially-made electronic buzzers primarily designed for carp fishing. A good night-fishing indicator should be sensitive and, most important, easy to see from any angle. This does not apply if a buzzer is used.

An extremely simple yet highly effective indicator can be made up at home from the following non-expensive materials:

(Fig. 7)

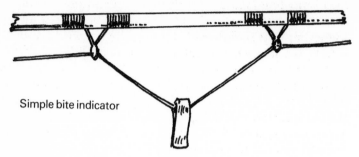

Simple bite indicator

the cork from a bottle; a 12 watt bulb; a yard of hearing-aid flex; two small jack plugs and a grid-bias battery. The cork should be cut and bored-out as in Fig. 8. The bulb should be soldered to the flex. The free ends of the flex should then be passed down through the bored-out section of the cork and the bulb neatly bedded down sideways-on into the waiting gap. A section of cork should then be fitted into the aperture above the bulb and glued firmly into place. When this is done, only the tip of the bulb should be showing and for added protection you should make certain that this does not protrude beyond the edge of the cork, otherwise the bulb may be broken in use or in transit. A slit should be made in the top of the cork with a razor blade and, finally, the jack plugs attached. The indicator is now ready to be plugged into the battery when required. By moving the jack plugs from one battery socket to another you can control the light output to suit your own requirements.

(Fig. 8)

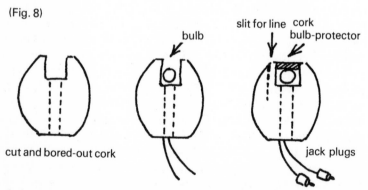

A simple home-made indicator for night fishing (see also Fig. 9)

In practice, I find only a slight glow is needed. When in use the fishing line should be clipped into the slit on the top of the cork, so that the exposed end of the bulb faces back along the rod towards the reel. Provided the line between rod tip and lead is tight the slightest mouthings of a hungry fish will cause the indicator to rise in a series of jerks (see **Fig. 9**). With an ordinary silver-paper indicator many of these preliminary pulls pass undetected but with an illuminated indicator the slightest pull on the line is clearly visible. Always make the indicator as light and as compact as possible, for a heavy indicator will alarm a taking fish and cause it to eject the bait.

(Fig. 9)

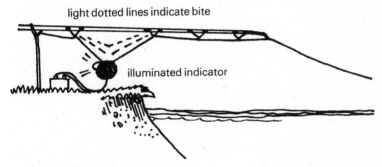

light dotted lines indicate bite

illuminated indicator

The home-made indicator in use

Bream seldom pick up a bait and make off holding it in their lips as carp do, instead they seem to pick it up and drop it two or three times before finally accepting it. Consequently bream bites on leger tackle seem to follow a set pattern. First the indicator will twitch several times and then, finally, it will move steadily up towards the rod. Then and only then should the strike be made. A premature strike will usually result in a complete miss. With a visible indicator every move of the fish can be carefully calculated but with an audible indicator it is very difficult to judge just what is going on. It is advisable to sit back and wait for a run to develop. Once this occurs the buzzer will make a continuous noise and a quick firm strike should lead to a hooked fish. Where bream are concerned I much prefer the illuminated indicator for night work as it gives a far more positive indication of a coming bite than does an electronic buzzer.

Methods

Float fishing

In swims of moderate depth, float tackle can be used to catch bream. It is rare, however, for float fishermen to catch very large bream; for these usually fall to leger tackle. As the bream is a bottom feeder, the laying-on technique (see Roach chapter) is the only really practical method of float fishing. Bream bites on float tackle are easy to see and nearly always follow a set pattern. Normally the first indication that a bream has found the bait comes when the float bobs sharply two or three times. After these preliminary knocks, the float usually lifts up and keels over as the bream picks up the bait and lifts the shot from the bottom (see Fig. 10). As a rule the float will tip right over and lie flat before sliding gently off over the surface, submerging as it goes. The strike should only be made when the float is moving off in this fashion.

Float fishing is only recommended for sport; anglers wishing to catch specimen bream will be well advised to stick to leger tackle.

(Fig. 10)

Typical bream bite, showing how the float 'lays' over as the bait is lifted from the bottom

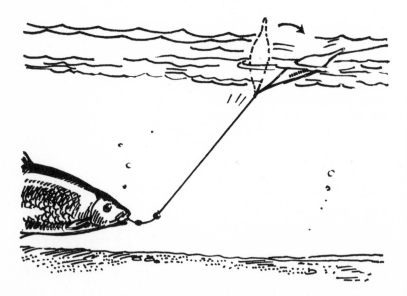

Legering

Being almost entirely a bottom-feeding fish, bream respond well to baits presented on leger tackle. This is fortunate for in deep water float-fishing, even with a sliding float, can be an extremely awkward technique to employ. The leger, however, is simple to set up, easy to cast and extremely sensitive in operation; which makes it the perfect terminal rig to use in deep water swims. For general bream fishing a plain free-running leger (see Fig. 11) can be used but on hard-fished waters, or where the bream are in a finicky mood, a more sensitive set of terminal tackle should be employed. The link leger (see Fig. 12) is ideal, for with the lead on a separate length of nylon, a

(Fig. 11)

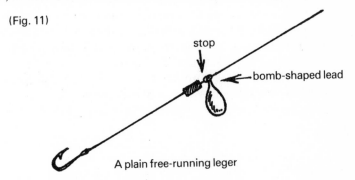

stop

bomb-shaped lead

A plain free-running leger

(Fig. 12)

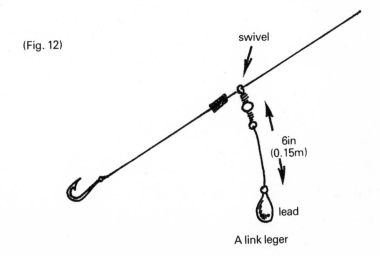

swivel

6in
(0.15m)

lead

A link leger

fish can pick up the bait and move a long way without feeling the weight of the lead at all. Bites on link-leger tackle are often firm, decisive affairs that are extremely easy to strike at. The distance between lead and hook depends a great deal on the water being fished. Only local experience can show you just what is required. On a new water start with about 18 in (45 cm) between hook and lead or hook and lead link. This can then be adjusted to suit the conditions of the water in question.

Block-end feeder

Bream respond well to most forms of groundbaiting but, at times, when the fish are being very cautious a standard block-end feeder (see Fig. 13) can be extremely useful for attracting fish to the vicinity of the bait. The block-end feeder comes in many shapes and sizes. Most tackle shops stock a variety of patterns. The best, in my opinion, is the Drennan feeder which was invented by an old friend, Peter Drennan of Oxford. The block-end feeder is constructed from a plastic cylinder (see Fig. 14), one end of which is sealed. The other end is capped to allow the introduction of maggots. The whole cylinder is perforated to allow the live maggots to wriggle out. To get the best out of a block-end feeder the hook should be no more than 6 in (15 cm) from the feeder (see Fig. 15). Fish of all kinds show no fear of the actual feeder. Instead they become so preoccupied with the escaping maggots that, hopefully, they pick up the maggot-baited hook in the process.

Used sensibly and at the right time a block-end feeder can be a real asset to the serious bream angler; used badly and without thought it can only be a drawback.

(Fig. 13)   A standard block-end feeder

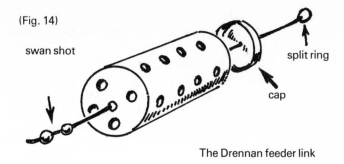

(Fig. 14)

swan shot

split ring

cap

The Drennan feeder link

(Fig. 15)

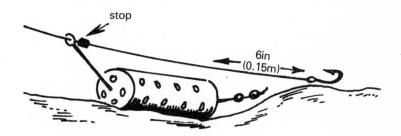

stop

6in
(0.15m)

The Drennan feeder link in use

Handling

Although bream have a thick protective coat of heavy slime, they are rather fragile fish and need to be handled with care. The fins and tail are particularly delicate and tend to split and fray very quickly. Also, the protective slime wears off very quickly exposing the small neat scales. Because of this fragility, it is essential to take great care when handling bream. Always make sure that your hands are wet before touching the fish.

Most important of all, make certain you never overcrowd bream in a keepnet as this probably does more permanent harm to the fish than anything else. When the bream are coming thick and fast it is easy to forget this and cram fish after fish into the keepnet without realising just how much damage is being inflicted upon them.

Anyone who has seen a really good catch of big bream tipped out of a keepnet will know how pitiful a sight these fish can be.

Gone are the neat well-made fins and tails; instead the fish are pathetic, ragged creatures in all probability doomed to a slow death from fungoid growth or some other disease. Even the biggest of keepnets is too small to contain more than one good bream at a time and even then the fish may be a little cramped. The *only* way to deal with this problem, if you want to retain all your bream, is to carry two or three large keepnets on all bream-fishing expeditions. Better still is to return all the smaller fish as they are caught. Keep only the biggest fish, which will naturally be few and far between. By doing this, little harm will come to the smaller stock-fish or to the big fish and this in turn will ensure that there will be plenty of healthy bream left to give sport in future seasons. Every bream angler can help this conservation effort, simply by purchasing a really big keepnet and using it sensibly.

Carp

Although the official record for carp still stands at 44 lb (20 kg) it is a well-established fact that top carp-angler Chris Yates caught a magnificent 51¼ lb (23.25 kg) carp from Redmire Pool: the same water, in fact, that produced the record-breaking 44 pounder. Angling politics have much to answer for regarding the status of the larger fish. The fact that this monster carp will never be accepted as the new record has raised a storm of controversy that will probably continue to rage for many years. I, and I think most anglers in this country, now look upon the Yates fish as the record carp, in spite of what the record-fish committee say on the subject. The fish was actually returned alive to the water soon after capture. Unfortunately, five months later it was found dead. Undoubtedly it was an extremely old fish.

The majority of carp in our waters are direct descendants of imported stock, most of which came from Europe; where fast-growing carp are now farmed commercially for eating purposes. Under ideal conditions these continental king carp have a growth rate of at least 3 lb (1.4 kg) per year, which makes them ideal stock fish. The variation in scale formation of these fish is too complicated to go into in detail and most anglers refer to them as mirror, leather or fully-scaled carp. The latter should not be confused with the old English or wild carp which will be described later in this section. The mirror carp gets its name from the large irregular scales said to resemble mirrors, which are scattered over its body. There are several distinct variations of mirror carp, some of which are extremely beautiful. The leather carp is practically devoid of scales and gets its name from its tough leathery skin.

Leather carp are less common than mirror carp, though by no means rare. The body colouring of carp varies considerably from one water to another. Normally the upper section of the body is dark blue, the flanks are chestnut, and the underparts yellow or almost orange. These colours vary from pale to exceptionally brilliant, depending on the quality of the water in which the fish live and the amount of food available. Rich waters usually produce the most attractive fish. Fully-scaled king carp are, of course, covered with neat attractive scales. These fish are usually bronze. The true carp is a short deep fish which has an extremely powerful appearance. Occasionally, in over-stocked waters which hold several generations of carp, the fish begin to revert to the wild form, losing their deep-bodied appearance and becoming long and lean in shape. A water that holds mirror or leather carp of this type is most unlikely to produce any really big fish.

Feeding habits

These fish are mostly found in lakes and they feed mainly during the summer, when they will often take food from the surface. Earlier in the season, they browse in the soft-weed beds, feeding among the new growth. As carp have a marked preference for water with weed, when they are found in rivers, it is usually somewhere having both weed and a slightly muddy bottom from which they can take water-snails, worms and larvae.

Baits

Worm, bread and maggots are the three main carp baits but they will also take potato, banana, green beans, peas, cheese, slugs and freshwater mussels.

Large lob or garden worms make excellent carp bait, used singly or in bunches. Small redworms or brandlings should be bunched so that they form a wriggling ball of food. As with bream, carp seem to find these almost irresistible, again possibly because the ball resembles a large mass of wriggling bloodworms.

Bread is still one of the most popular carp baits. It can be used in a variety of ways. A paste made of stale bread and water makes a excellent bait. This should be used in lumps the size of a golf ball. Flake is another good carp bait. This consists simply of bait-sized portions of the inside of a new loaf, pinched round the shank of the hook, leaving a fluffy natural section of bread round the point and bend of the hook (see Fig. 16). The flake should never be pinched round the point of the hook, for it will go hard in the water and may mask the hook point when the strike is made.

(Fig. 16)

Flaked bread makes an excellent carp bait

A matchbox-sized crust bait can be deadly. This is a surface bait which should be used close to the bank or round weed beds. A mixture of crust and bread paste (see Fig. 17) is a useful bait to employ when fishing over a weedy bottom. These balanced baits sink slowly and rest on top of the weed, instead of sinking into the weed as paste will do.

(Fig. 17)

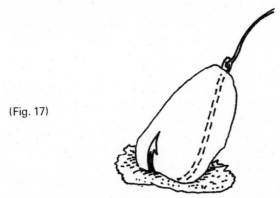

A balanced bait of paste and breadcrust will sink slowly, which makes it useful when fishing over a weedy bottom

On waters which are inundated with small fish the one bait which the carp angler can use with confidence is a small cooked potato. Although attractive to carp this is tough enough to withstand the mouthings of roach or rudd. Small new potatoes make the best baits. These should be boiled, until they just dent when squeezed between the thumb and forefinger. Tinned new potatoes can also be used. The only practical method of baiting up with a potato is to thread it on to the line with a baiting needle (see Fig. 18).

(Fig. 18)

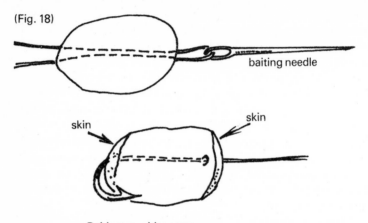

baiting needle

skin   skin

Baiting up with potato

Modern carp anglers are having considerable success with particle baits such as tinned sweetcorn, cooked beans, peas, tares, etc. Sweetcorn has proved the most successful of these baits. Sweetcorn grains can be used as single or multiple baits. I have caught big carp on a single grain of corn and on a bait consisting of six grains crammed onto a size 2 hook (see Fig. 19).

Carp are quick to learn fear. Most carp waters are hard fished and the carp quickly learn to associate certain baits with danger. This then has led to the development and use of 'special' baits. Some of which are worthy of mention.

(Fig. 19)

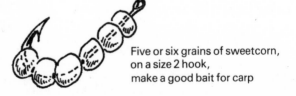

Five or six grains of sweetcorn, on a size 2 hook, make a good bait for carp

Special baits

Carp fishing has become a highly competitive sport. Top carp anglers have now reached the stage where they will divulge their 'secret' bait ingredient to no one. This may sound stupid but on hard-fished waters, where the carp have been caught many times on conventional baits, only special baits will catch fish. Once a secret bait compound becomes general knowledge the fish become wary again and a new bait has to be devised. The real carp fanatics use all manner of ingredients to flavour baits. A common mixture is crushed trout-food pellets and tinned cat food with an amino acid additive. This creates a high-protein mixture and has accounted for many monster carp. On waters where carp have become all too well aware that floating bread contains a hook, it is common practice to use cat biscuits as a substitute for floating breadcrust. In their normal state cat biscuits are too hard and brittle. To overcome this, carp anglers immerse the biscuits in boiling water for exactly 60 seconds. This turns the biscuits rubbery and in this state they make ideal surface baits.

Groundbaits

Loose grains of corn can be used as groundbait. Last year I had great success with cooked broadbeans as bait. The water I was fishing held a good head of wild carp in the 4–8 lb (1.8–3.6 kg) class and I pre-baited the swim for a fortnight prior to fishing. Result a good bag of nice average carp.

Location

Surface-feeding carp are easy to locate as the loud sucking noise they make quickly pinpoints their whereabouts. A string of fine bubbles rising from the bottom of a carp water also indicates that carp are in the swim and are browsing along the bottom. Carp also love to bask in the sun and can often be seen in the shallows. Locating carp is usually no problem; catching them is a far more difficult proposition.

Tackle

Rods

Carp rods have changed considerably in the past few years. The advent of carbon fibre and the constant improvement of fibreglass rod-blanks has led to a wide range of rods being manu-factured. Most of the better class rods are 11 ft (3.3 m) two piece weapons of 1½ or 2½ lb (0.7 or 1.1 kg) test curve. A 1½ lb (0.7 kg) test-curve rod is designed for handling lines of between 7 and 12 lb (3.2 and 5.4 kg) breaking strain while a 2½ lb (1.1 kg) rod will comfortably handle lines of up to 16 lb (7.2 kg) breaking strain. The heavier rods are designed for carp fishing in weedy waters or where heavy leads have to be used to achieve long casts. It is interesting to note that the controversial fore-mentioned 51¼ lb (23.25 kg) carp was caught on an original split-cane carp rod designed by master carp angler Richard Walker.

Reels

A medium-sized fixed-spool reel is best for general carp fishing, although for close-range work a centre-pin reel can be used quite comfortably. These latter reels are most suited for use with light lines; for float fishing close to the bank a good-quality centre pin cannot be bettered. Chris Yates who caught the huge carp swears by an Avon Royal Eagle reel made by Grice and Young.

Lines

Although the current record carp was caught on braided nylon line, very few carp anglers still use lines of this type and mono-filament lines are now the most popular. There are many brands of nylon available but not all are of high quality. Buying the best is usually cheapest in the long run and lines like Maxima, Platil and Sylcass are the brands most used by today's carp anglers. Line colour depends on personal preference. Brown, black or dark-green lines being less visible in the water than some of the blue and sand-coloured lines.

Hooks

There is, as yet, no such thing as a perfect carp hook although some good patterns are available. Carp are strong, leathery-mouthed fish, consequently a carp hook should have both strength and sharpness. This combination is a difficult thing to achieve, for to be strong the hook has to be thick in the wire and a thick-wired hook is difficult to sharpen. Jack Hilton or the

Lion D'Or hooks are ideal in many ways, being incredibly strong and having a good shape, but they have to be carefully sharpened before use.

A carborundum stone should be used to sharpen the hook point. Sizes 2 and 4 are the most useful hooks for all-round carp fishing but for extra-big baits a size 1–0 can be used. Always remember that large hooks lack the penetration of smaller patterns, so it is advisable to strike far harder than normal when an extra-big hook is being used.

Landing nets

Even a medium-sized carp is a big fish and a big landing net is an essential item of carp-fishing equipment. Special carp landing-net frames fitted with extra-deep net mesh can be purchased in most good tackle shops.

Carp and keepnets

Several outsize keepnets are now being marketed as carp nets. Despite the size and depth of these nets, they are still far from suitable for retaining carp. It is well known that carp do not take kindly to nets and instead of settling down like most other fish they will continually try to break through the confining mesh, suffering a great deal of damage in the process. Because of this, keepnets have been banned on most club and syndicate carp fisheries. There was one well-fished carp pool where the fish were being caught minus tails, fins and even scales, all due to their being kept in nets over long periods of time. Some of the carp from this water were in such a pitiful condition that they had to be destroyed. This state of affairs should be a warning to any carp angler who is considering using a keepnet to hold captured carp. Thinking anglers use a specially constructed carp sack made from knotless micro-mesh netting. These sacks are soft and therefore do no damage to the captured fish. They are cheap to buy and are obtainable from all good tackle shops.

Carp can be kept overnight in a sack and will suffer no ill-effects from this enforced confinement but never keep a fish you have caught for longer than is absolutely necessary and, wherever possible, weigh or photograph the fish as soon as it is caught and then return it immediately to the water.

For daylight carp fishing, audible bite indicators are not really necessary; for night fishing they are indispensable. There are many patterns available, most of which are powered by torch batteries. Some work on the antenna principle (see Fig. 20). The line is hooked behind the antenna, so that as soon as a fish takes the bait the movement of the line pulls the antenna across, making electrical contact which automatically makes the buzzer work. Others work on a roller system or on photo-electric cells.

(Fig. 20)

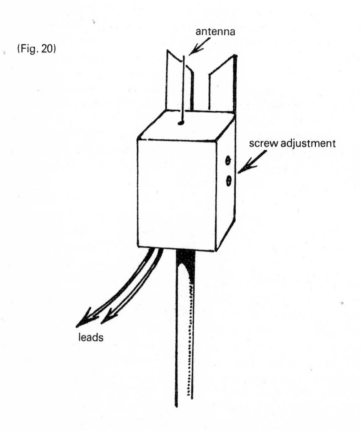

antenna

screw adjustment

leads

Simple audible bite indicator

Methods

Float fishing

In clear, rich waters carp often become pre-occupied with minute aquatic insects and will ignore the more conventional carp baits, including large worms. When this occurs, the angler must use a natural bait that bears a close resemblance to the larvae and nymphs upon which the carp are feeding. The only easily obtainable bait that falls into this category is the maggot, which bears a close resemblance to a caddis grub. Unfortunately maggots are small baits and require small hooks. Consequently, it is necessary to fish with a fine line and light rod when maggot-fishing for carp, and because of this many anglers will not use maggots as bait. This is a mistake, for these grubs are without doubt one of the deadliest of all known carp baits, even though they do not conform to the generally accepted theory of big baits for big fish. The Avon-styled trotting rod is ideal, as its easy, progressive action makes it suitable for handling light lines, setting hooks and playing big fish. These rods can be used in conjunction with a fixed-spool or centre-pin reel and 4 or 5 lb (1.8 or 2.3 kg) bs line. This is little more than roach tackle and a great deal of patience and skill is required to subdue and land big fish on tackle of this calibre.

Float fishing is the most enjoyable and often the most productive method of presenting a maggot bait for, although many carp anglers fish with floatless, leadless tackle, carp seem to show little fear of a float if it is used intelligently. Maggots seem to work best when used in deepish water close to the bank.

Carp are mainly bottom feeders and, to be most effective, the maggot bait should lie right on the pit bed. The laying-on method is ideal for this form of fishing and can usually be relied upon to produce results. Only very light and streamlined floats should be used and for all-round work a small antenna float is recommended (see Fig. 21). These floats have great stability and ride steadily in the roughest of water. To make the float even more stable and also ultra-sensitive, attach by the bottom end only. The float should be set so that at least a foot (30 cm) of line lies on the bottom. Providing that one or two of the shot also rest on the bottom, the float will show no tendency to drift.

For maggot fishing, small but strong hooks are essential. Inferior hooks will snap or straighten under pressure. One of the

(Fig. 21)

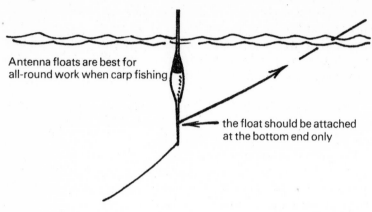

Antenna floats are best for
all-round work when carp fishing

the float should be attached
at the bottom end only

neatest and strongest of the small hooks is the Sundridge Specimen hook. A size 12 is suitable for maggots, which can be used either singly or in bunches depending upon the ever-changing moods of the fish. It is advisable to groundbait your swim with an occasional handful of loose maggots.

Although carp are regarded as nocturnal feeders, they can be caught at all times of the day, particularly on small natural baits like the maggot. Bites are normally registered by the float bobbing two or three times before sliding away across the surface. Great care must be taken when playing big carp on light tackle and the angler must be prepared at all times to yield line to the fish. Any attempt to force the pace will result in a broken line. No attempt should be made to net the carp until it is thoroughly subdued, otherwise it may make a last desperate (and often successful) attempt to escape.

Legering

Carp respond well to baits presented on leger tackle. Many of today's carp anglers dispense entirely with leger leads and rely entirely on the weight of the bait for casting purposes. Even light worm baits can be cast quite a distance and large balls of bread paste or whole potato baits can be cast even further without undue effort.

When legering for carp, or for any other freshwater fish, two rod rests are essential. Great care should be taken to ensure that the rests are set so that a taking fish can pull line from the reel without feeling any resistance to its movements. By setting the front rod-rest slightly lower than the back rest, it is possible to ensure that the line can run freely at all times. Never set the rests so that the rod tip points up, as a biting fish will then have to pull the rod tip down before it can take line, and no self-respecting carp will do that without immediately rejecting the bait!

Legering is the simplest of all methods to use and at the same time it is the best method to employ; more carp fall to the leadless leger than to any other technique.

For ultra long-range fishing a leger lead can be used, but on waters where carp are tackle-shy the use of a lead may well result in the fish ignoring the bait. I much prefer to fish a weightless leger at all times.

Stalking carp

One of the most exciting and productive methods of taking big carp during the daytime is to stalk the fish as they lie basking in the sun. This requires a great deal of patience and stealth and accurate casting is essential. Where possible it is advisable to try only for fish that bask in the openings between weed beds, for the weeds give the angler added cover and the carp seem to show less caution when surrounded by thick weed.

The only baits that can be used for this form of carp fishing are breadcrusts and cat biscuits, as these baits will float even when saturated with water. Other baits sink immediately and are useless. A crust bait the size of a thumbnail is ideal and should be used with a size 2 short-shanked hook. Quite a large portion of the hook point and bend must project from the crust (see Fig. 22), for with this form of carp fishing the strike should be made immediately the carp sucks in the bait. If the hook is buried in the crust it may fail to penetrate when the strike is made.

(Fig. 22)

The floating crust method is an excellent way of stalking carp

Basking carp are simple to locate, for their large size and dark blue backs make them distinctive even when surrounded by thick weed. Once a fish is spotted, it is necessary to get within casting range without disturbing it. This takes practice but providing the operation is not hurried in any way it is fairly simple to get close to the unsuspecting fish. Under no circumstances should the crust be cast directly at the fish, as the resulting splash will frighten it. Instead the bait should be cast to fall several yards/metres beyond the fish, then slowly drawn back until it is floating close to its snout. The fish will often gulp down the bait within seconds of its arrival but occasionally the fish will ignore it completely. If this occurs the crust should be twitched slightly. This unusual and unnatural movement will sometimes infuriate the carp to such a degree that it will take the crust in a most decisive manner. As it is possible to watch every movement the fish makes, a firm fast strike should be made as soon as its mouth closes over the bait. Any delay may give the fish time to eject the bait and make off. Provided that the fish does not sense the presence of the angler it will usually take the bait with confidence. The hotter the day the more chance of sport, for carp seem to lose their caution on really warm days. This is an exciting but difficult form of fishing.

Suspended crust method

This is a highly effective technique which will often catch carp when all the more conventional methods fail to produce results. Suspended crust tackle is set up in the same way as a standard running leger, the weight being just sufficient to anchor the crust bait which being buoyant will rise as far as the trail between lead and hook will allow (see Fig. 23). This method works best in shallow water and the tackle should be arranged so that the crust is suspended at mid-water level. This simply means that in a swim that is 5 ft (1.5 m) deep the lead should be stopped 2½ ft (75 cm) from the hook leaving a trail 30 in (75 cm) long. Although a crust fixed in this way looks unnatural, carp seem to find it attractive and on hard-fished waters where the carp are known to be extremely line-shy the suspended crust method is most useful, for the fish do not notice the line beneath the crust and often take the bait firmly without any preliminary mouthings. This method works well during the day and also at night.

44

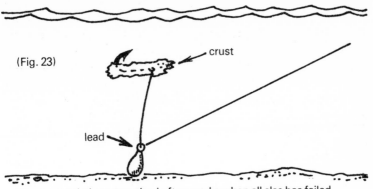

(Fig. 23)

crust

lead

The suspended crust method often works when all else has failed

Suspended worm method

This is a technique used to catch carp when they are feeding beneath floating lily pads. Unlike the suspended crust method, no lead should be used; the weight of the worm being sufficient for casting purposes. This is essentially a daylight technique and one that produces excellent results if used correctly. There can be no question of actually casting the worm to a specific fish. Instead the bait should be cast so that it hangs suspended over a lily pad, in a likely spot. Once in position the bait must be left alone to wriggle and twist just beneath the surface. Any attempt to move the bait will result in the hook catching in the lily leaves. Carp respond well to worms fished in this manner and probably regard them as completely natural objects: carp suck a great deal of natural food from the undersides of lily leaves and are unlikely to pass up a worm without attempting to take it, particularly as the line will be hidden by the leaves.

Fishing the margins

Big carp are creatures of habit and unless disturbed will frequent certain areas regularly. They are particularly fond of patrolling the marginal shallows in search of food and because of this the technique known as *margin fishing* has evolved. This is a most exciting and for the fish often deadly form of angling which requires great patience on the part of the angler. Floating bread crust is the most widely used margin-fishing bait, for oddments of bread often collect close to the bank and carp quickly learn that they can pick an easy living by regularly visiting the bankside swims in search of food. Swims with a screen of reeds lend themselves to margin fishing as the reeds hide the angler from the view of the fish and, equally as important, break up the straight and unnatural outline of the rod.

Once the tackle is set up and the crust lowered on to the surface great care must be taken to make no further movement for carp are ultra-sensitive fish and the slightest movement on the part of the angler will create enough vibration to frighten any carp in the swim. The line between rod tip and bait should be kept fairly taut as carp are quick to notice loose coils of floating line and will leave a bait strictly alone if they sense that all is not well. At the same time a slight amount of slack should be left, otherwise even a gentle breeze might cause the rod tip to sway which, in turn, might cause the crust to move and ripple the water. A bait that does this will never catch a fish. Very occasionally, the first indication that a fish is in the swim comes when the bait is suddenly sucked down without prior warning. More often than not, however, the fish will give itself away by making loud sucking noises or by creating ripples as it browses slowly into the swim. Sometimes a cautious fish will spend a considerable amount of time trying to overcome its fear and take the bait. Fish like this have usually been caught before and have learned to associate a bait with danger. Carp are quick to spit out a suspect bait, and when margin fishing, where a fish can move only a few inches/several centimetres with the bait in its mouth before feeling the drag of the rod tip, the angler must be ready to strike as soon as the bait is taken.

Although most carp fishermen use floating breadcrust baits for margin fishing, worms, paste or potato baits can also be used. These should be fished right on the bottom and close to the bank, and are best used during cool, windy weather when water temperatures are low.

Carp fishing in winter

Carp fishing traditionally finishes in late September or early October and few fishermen bother to try to catch carp again until the following June; the belief being that carp go into hibernation with the onset of winter and do not emerge until late March or early April when the water temperatures begin to rise. To some extent this is true but there are times, even in the middle of winter, when the fish temporarily come out of hibernation. This normally occurs during periods of sunny weather when the sunlight penetrates the water for prolonged periods. After the end of January carp often become extremely active, and the last six weeks of the season can be most productive.

Even at its best, carp fishing is a slow pastime and, as might be expected, winter carp fishing is no exception. It is obviously not possible to go carp fishing at *any* time during the winter months and expect to catch fish, but by fishing on the brighter days it is sometimes possible to secure a good fish. Although, even on apparently ideal days many blank trips may be recorded before a carp is caught. I remember one bright winter's day when I took three fine carp in the space of two hours and then did not take another for the remainder of the winter months.

Handling carp

Big king carp being pot-bellied are easily ruptured. To avoid this happening all fish should be handled very carefully, and jerky movements should be avoided. When returning a carp to the water, always lower the fish gently into the swim and give it time to recover before finally releasing it. Under no circumstances should a fish be dropped or thrown back into the water. Carp have tough leathery mouths and to avoid tearing the lips it is advisable to cut the line and pull the hook through shank first. This is a quicker and more humane method than the normal technique where the point and barb of the hook has to be worked out of the lips by force.

Artery forceps can be used to unhook carp and other big fish. These instruments are extremely useful and can be purchased from any good tackle dealer.

Crucian Carp

The crucian carp is probably the most neglected fish in the British Isles.

Its inbred shyness and its secretive habits make it a difficult fish to catch in any quantity. Because of this, and because of its small average size when compared with the more popular mirror and common carp, few anglers ever seriously fish for crucian carp; and those fish that are caught and recorded usually fall to baits intended for roach or rudd. Crucian carp have rather a limited distribution, although they are probably more common than most anglers realise.

By nature the crucian carp is a still-water species, mostly found in long established weedy lakes. Many clubs are now carrying out extensive restocking programmes and the crucian carp is one of the species being used to repopulate club-owned waters. They are attractive fish, with neat scales, bronze sides and long convex dorsal fins. Although comparatively small they have a powerful look, and often fight extremely well when hooked. Crucian carp vary considerably in size from one water to another and because of this it is difficult to say what weight a crucian carp has to attain before it can be regarded as a specimen. Obviously in waters which hold thousands upon thousands of crucian carp weighing 8–12 oz (0.22–0.34 kg) a 16 oz (0.45 kg) fish is a specimen. In other waters where the average weight of fish is higher, a crucian of 2 lb (0.9 kg) or more is a specimen. This latter is generally regarded as a good weight where these fish are concerned and anything over 3 lb (1.4 kg) is regarded as an excellent catch. The crucian carp record is held by a fish weighing 4 lb 11 oz (2.12 kg). Few other crucian carp over 4 lb (1.8 kg) have been caught.

Crucian carp, like the common carp, are basically a summer species which sink into a torpid or semi-torpid state during the colder months. Occasionally a big crucian carp is caught by a winter angler, usually on a bright sunny day when the water's temperature has risen a few degrees. Few anglers, however, seriously fish for crucian carp after the end of September and those that are caught are taken by accident on bait intended for other fish.

Feeding habits

These are very similar to those of the common carp and although both fish are bottom feeders they also have a passion for food taken from the underside of leaves.

Baits

Crucian carp can be caught on all the standard roach baits including worms. Maggots are the most popular, for they are both natural and easy to obtain in quantity. These grubs can be used singly or in bunches, depending upon the varying moods of the fish concerned.

Bread crust, paste or flake from a new loaf are likely to tempt the biggest crucian carp and when the fish are on the feed a ragged piece of flake pinched on to the shank of the hook can be deadly. This can be made even more attractive to the fish by threading several maggots on to the bend of the hook. These combination baits are little used as yet in this country but are extremely effective under most conditions, and can often be relied upon to produce bites when all the more conventional baits have failed to arouse the interest of the fish.

Brandlings and small lively redworms are also extremely good as crucian carp bait, although rarely used by most anglers; probably because they are more difficult to come by than maggots and more messy to use. Worm baits, even when scoured for a few days in moss are rather soft, and unless the strike is made at the first definite indication of a bite, the carp will probably manage to tear the worm off the hook.

I have also caught some very big crucian carp in recent seasons on a worm-sweetcorn combination bait.

Groundbait

Crucian carp respond well to groundbait and where possible a swim should be thoroughly pre-baited well in advance. Any light sausage, rusk or bran-based groundbait is suitable and can be made even more attractive by the addition of maggots and whole or chopped worms. A few handfuls of groundbait introduced during the time actually spent fishing can also attract and hold the attention of the fish, and it always pays to carry a small supply of groundbait when after crucian carp.

Location

Unlike the other types of carp, the crucian is a shoal fish which means that when one is caught there are usually others in the swim. Obviously the size of the shoal depends on the individual size of the fish it contains, and the largest shoals normally consist of small and medium-sized crucian carp.

The big fish live and feed in small groups, which may contain less than a dozen individuals. Because of this, it is very rare to catch really big bags of specimen crucian carp. Crucian carp love weed, particularly of the surface type for this gives them cover, shade and also provides them with a great deal of natural food in the form of insects, small water snails and water-snail eggs which they suck from the underside of the floating leaves. This habit often gives the fish away, for the movement of the weed and the loud sucking noises, are a sure indication that crucian carp are in a swim. Crucian carp also like to leap out of the water and this helps pinpoint the whereabouts of a shoal.

The best crucian-carp swims are normally situated beside dense weed beds. When visiting a water for the first time, an angler after crucian carp will be well advised to seek out a swim that contains either surface or bottom weed and fish it hard. In waters that contain little or no weed, location of fish can be far more difficult and in many cases it becomes a matter for trial and error. Crucian carp feed well when the water temperature is high. At these times shallow swims normally fish the best. When water temperature is low, due to inclement weather or high wind, the fish move to the deeper water in search of food and the wise angler will move his or her pitch accordingly.

Tackle

Although crucian carp are game and sporting fish, they can be subdued quite easily on light tackle. Consequently a standard roach-fishing outfit can be used with confidence for the majority of crucian carp fishing (see Roach chapter), although a slightly more substantial set of tackle is useful for fishing in heavily-weeded swims. An Avon-type trotting rod is recommended for this sort of work, used in conjunction with a line of 3 or 4 lb (1.4 or 1.8 kg) breaking strain, so that a fish hooked in the densest part of the swim can be forced out of the weed without fear of smashing the tackle in the process.

Hooks

Crucian carp have small mouths and show a marked preference for small baits, so there is no need to use a hook larger than size 8. The size of hook used depends on the type of bait employed. As a rough guide, the following recommendations give a fair indication of the most suitable hook sizes for the various baits which attract crucian carp. For maggot fishing size 14 or 16 hooks are best; for worms or small bread baits size 10 and 12; for larger bread baits, large worms or combination baits a size 8 hook should be used.

Methods

Float fishing

Crucian carp are shy-biting fish, noted for the delicate way in which they take a bait. Because of this, most crucian carp anglers use only the lightest of float tackle and even then many bites pass unnoticed. More than one angler has started to bring in his tackle and found himself firmly hooked into a large crucian carp that had managed to take his bait without making the float even tremble in the process. Crucian carp are generally regarded as bottom feeders but will also feed well off the surface, particularly when the water temperatures are high. Because of this it is sometimes advisable to fish with a self-cocking float (see Rudd chapter), so that the bait sinks slowly and naturally. With this sort of terminal tackle bites are often easier to detect as the fish usually take the bait more decisively and then run with it, so that the float slides off across the surface gradually submerging as it goes. This is a technique that often catches crucian carp of specimen size. Only a tiny quill float should be used for this kind of fishing. Patches of open water, among thick beds of surface weed, are ideal places to use this method. Maggots or worms make the most suitable baits, for they are both light and natural in appearance and, providing the swim remains undisturbed, the fish take these baits with confidence.

Legering

Under certain conditions legering can be an extremely effective way of catching crucian carp; for night fishing or long-range work it is the only practical method to employ. A conventional leger employing a free-running lead weight can only be used in swims that are weed free, for in weedy swims the weight of the lead will pull the bait into the weed and hide it from the carp. Even in weed-free swims only the smallest leads should be used, preferably on a sliding link so that a taking fish can move away freely without feeling any check to its movement.

Legering as a technique is as yet little used by crucian carp fishermen, despite the fact that these small carp respond well to leger tackle.

Night fishing

Traditionally late evening and dawn are the most productive times to go crucian carp fishing. To some extent this is true, although crucian carp also feed well throughout the night and the angler who begins to fish in the late evening or at dawn is taking advantage only of the beginning and the end of the carps' feeding period.

True carp dislike artificial light and will often stop feeding at the slightest flash from a torch. Crucian carp do not seem to share this fear and many anglers use a strong torch to illuminate their swim at night. The only advantage to be gained from this is that a float can be used instead of a leger. The full beam of the lamp should *never* be pointed directly into the water. Instead the light should be aimed across the swim so that the main glare does not penetrate beneath the surface. When a torch is used in this way to illuminate a shallow swim, crucian carp can often be seen crossing and re-crossing the illuminated area. Many fishermen dislike the use of light at night and object strongly if a torch is employed to illuminate a swim, for this reason a torch should only be used when it does not interfere with other anglers.

Chub

Although the chub is rather a long fish, it gives the impression of bulk. The head, in particular, is large as are the scales and tail. In the adult fish the colour is silver with a distinct gold or bronze tint. The back varies from green to almost black and both the dorsal and caudal fins are grey. The underside of the fish is white, with either a pale watery red or a brilliant crimson hue to the pectoral, pelvic and anal fins.

The Hampshire Avon was once noted as the best chub water in England. Unfortunately, Avon chub became infested with an internal parasite which to some degree ruined the river as a chub water.

Depending on the amount of food available, chub have a fair growth rate and although 5 lb (2.3 kg) is a good fish, it is by no means a real specimen. The record at present is held by a 7 lb 6 oz (3.34 kg) fish which came from the Hampshire Avon.

Chub can be found in many running waters over most of Great Britain, and I now know of several south-country gravel pits that hold fish of huge size.

Feeding habits

Although omnivorous, chub will accept a livebait sooner than a dead or stale offering. Where and when chub feed depends entirely on the amount and type of food available at the time and place and they will quickly become preoccupied with certain food. For instance, if there is a heavy hatch of fly then the chub will gorge themselves on insects and completely ignore any other offering. It is this trait that will occasionally bring about their downfall. For the angler can, by the judicious use of groundbait, woo them into accepting a baited hook.

Chub believe in a varied diet! They are known to accept worms, maggots, bread, cheese (the riper the better), slugs, sausage, luncheon meat, hempseed or elderberries, live fish, dead fish, macaroni, wheat and crayfish – in fact anything they can find – provided, as a rule, that it does not contain a hook. One or two baits may need a little explanation. Cheese, for instance, can either be mixed with bread and turned into a paste, or it can be used as a cube. If a cheese cube is used then it pays to rub down the corners, to round them off a little, so that a feeding fish can get the offering well inside its mouth.

Chub will often accept a fat slug in preference to another bait. Slugs, of course, are easy to collect but unpleasant to handle. Most anglers use a pair of artery forceps to pick up and bait up with slug. Slugs are usually fished on the freeline principle, no weight on the line, just the weight of the bait being used for casting purposes. Chub usually take a freelined slug with a bang, dragging the tip of the rod hard round in the process. Such bites are difficult to miss on the strike.

Crayfish make excellent chub bait, provided they have been found in the water that is to be fished. Most chub anglers use them whole, on leadless, floatless tackle, the bait being mounted head down so that it gives a life-like appearance. Crayfish are found mainly where streams or rivers run through clay. They burrow into the soft soil and can be extracted quite easily, but be careful not to push your hand into the hole of a water vole by mistake!

Another way to catch crayfish is to lay the head of a landing net, suitably baited with a piece of fish, on the bottom of a swim and then haul it up at regular intervals to extract the crayfish.

Few anglers like the idea of impaling a live fish on a hook and because of this deadbaiting is becoming increasingly popular; for by using dead fish as bait any angler can fish with a natural bait without causing pain to a live creature.

On a number of occasions I have known chub to accept a legered deadbait; bleak or small gudgeon seem to be best. These dead baits should be mounted in the same manner as an eel bait (see Eel chapter). During the winter of 1981 some huge chub were caught from a gravel pit in Oxfordshire on pike-size deadbait. Fish to 7 lb 2 oz (3.23 kg) were taken on whole mackerel, proof of the size of bait that a chub can swallow.

There is obviously tremendous potential for deadbait fishing for big chub and it would seem that in time the use of large deadbaits will come to be regarded as a normal part of chub fishing.

Tackle

Rods

I use an Alan Brown 11 ft 4 in (3.45 m) trotting rod when float fishing for chub. This rod is perfect for this form of fishing. For leger work I prefer a two piece 10 ft (3 m) MkIV Avon-style rod. This is light enough to be held at all times, yet powerful enough to cast a big bait or set a large hook.

Reels

For fast-water float fishing a centre-pin reel will prove to be the most useful but for legering, or small-water chub hunting, a fixed-spool reel will be invaluable.

Lines

I seldom use anything lighter than 5 lb (2.3 kg) breaking strain for chub and where the water is much overgrown this line strength can be stepped up to 7 lb (3.2 kg).

Hooks

A chub has a large mouth and a small hook will, nine times out of ten, pull straight out on the strike. So it is wise to use a size 6 or 8 for float work and a size 2 or 4 carp hook for leger work; the exception being when small baits are used. For maggots or sweetcorn I use a size 12 or 14 hook. Hooks that are smaller than this should be avoided, as a good size chub is a strong fighter and can easily straighten a small hook.

Floats

Most float fishing for chub is done on fast waters, where a large float is needed to enable the bait to be trotted well downstream to the fish. Even though a big cork-bodied or balsa-bodied float is needed, do not sacrifice the sensitivity of such a float. Always keep the body as streamlined as possible, so that it offers little or no resistance when the chub finally takes the bait. Fortunately, there are now many fine trotting floats available, some of the best being made by Peter Drennen of Oxford. Peter is a top angler who has brought his expertise to the tackle-making business. His floats are no-nonsense masterpieces. Long before going into commercial float production Peter made floats for anglers such as Richard Walker, Peter Stone, Fred Taylor and myself.

Leger leads

As always these should be the smallest size that will satisfactorily serve the required purpose.

Methods

Float fishing

When the strength of the current will allow it, long trotting provides an effective and pleasant way of catching fish. It is not, however, an easy style to master and calls for great skill where tackle control is concerned, as well as sound river knowledge. One of the most important advantages of long trotting is that it enables the angler to sit well-back, upstream of the fish. This is essential, for chub are cautious in the extreme and will rapidly fade from view at the slightest disturbance. The angler must be constantly on the alert, for bites can come from any part of the swim and are usually so sudden that, unless the angler is concentrating, the fish will have taken and ejected the bait in a matter of seconds. The strike must be made as soon as the float starts to dip; and the angler must keep in direct contact with the float (the further away the tackle is, the harder the strike must be), otherwise the angler will be too slow to hook the taking fish.

Chub fishing is a roving game, and it is wise to carry only the tackle you need so that you can quickly move on to another swim without too much inconvenience.

Legering

If the fish are well out of reach of normal float tackle the only answer is to leger. I find that in summer I consistently catch fish on the rolling-bait style while in winter a static leger is more efficient.

Dapping

During the summer months chub sometimes rise to the surface

to lie soaking up the warmth of the sun. Yet, even at a time like this, they seldom venture far from their retreats among the tree roots or overhanging vegetation. These top-water chub seldom feed in the accepted sense of the word, but they can be tempted to take a live insect from the surface, provided that it arrives in front of them in a natural manner and so long as they do not suspect it to be attached to a hook. This method is not as difficult as it sounds, provided that the angler takes great care when approaching the swim and does not frighten the fish by any sudden movement. The type of swim that lends itself to this approach is one that lies underneath an overhanging tree, so that the insect appears to have just fallen from the branches.

The tree trunk will also serve to hide the angler from the fish's view. Any insect will do for bait, but a grasshopper, if obtainable, will prove more attractive to chub than any other lure.

Spinning

Chub eat a fair proportion of small fish and a chub will often succumb to the lure of a small fly-spoon or minnow, especially if you throw caution to the winds and spin the bait as close as possible to the chub's haunt.

Fly fishing

Chub respond well to artificial flies and, as long as they do not become suspicious they will rise again and again to a fly. Chub flies are more successful if they are tied on largish hooks so that, although the pattern is say an Alder or a Zulu, they are at least four times the normal size. Big and 'buzzy' is the rule when fishing for chub.

Whether the fly be dry or wet does not matter, as chub will happily accept anything that resembles an insect.

Floating crust

A piece of crust floated down across a chub hole will sometimes tempt a fish. If the chub are known to lie underneath a raft of floating branches, twigs and other river debris, the crust should be cast out so that it comes to rest on the edge of the debris; frequently a chub will rise and take the bait although whether or not you are able to entice the fish from its stronghold is entirely a matter of luck.

57

General advice

If the chub continually ignore a bait trotted or rolled straight past them, they can sometimes be tempted to take it if the bait is cast so that it drops just behind their tails. I am not sure why this happens, but it may be that the fish are jealous of another member of the shoal getting to the bait first.

Chub anglers often cast right over, under the opposite bank, completely ignoring the fish that live almost beneath their feet. These under-the-rod-tip chub can be caught quite easily if the swim is approached cautiously.

Winter chub

Once the colder weather sets in and the first floods flush away all the summer weed-growth, chub will move away from their summer haunts and seek out the more sheltered swims, well away from the full force of the winter currents. As a rule they do not move far and the angler should look for the quieter water, close to the swims that held chub in the summer. It is in such places that the chub congregate and feed on the worms and insects that flood water brings to them.

Cold weather tactics

Winter chub appear to have a distinct preference for worm baits. Size does not seem important, and I have known chub take both lobworms and small redworms in consecutive casts. If, however, a real freeze-up sets in, then the fish may be inclined to take a piece of crust or a bunch of maggots fished on a static leger.

Cold-water chub are disinclined to move far in search of food; consequently I find they completely ignore a bait that wavers in the current but will quickly take one that lies completely still, so the lead must be stopped close to the hook leaving only a short trace of 3 or 4 in (7.5-10 cm).

Bites on this kind of tackle are usually registered as a gentle pluck instead of the usual hard pull of a summer fish. This occurs because, instead of picking up the bait and immediately turning away downstream with it, the cold-water chub will eat it on the spot. So strike at the tiniest tremble and the chub should be on. Do not, however, wait for that definite heavy pull, for it may never come.

By far the most fascinating form of chub fishing is 'chasing' the fish on small, overgrown waters. The tackle should be kept as simple as possible with no float or lead and the hook should be tied directly to the reel line with just the weight of the bait to aid casting. It is very easy to frighten fish on smaller waters, and great stealth is needed to creep up to a position from which the bait can be dropped over the top of the bank, or gently cast up under a dark tunnel of overhanging vegetation. If a bite is forthcoming it is usually within a minute or so of the cast, but it pays to leave the bait longer if necessary.

Once a fish is hooked, it should not be played but dragged out away from obstructions. Once the fish is in comparatively open water you can ease up the pressure a little. As there is no finesse in this kind of chub catching, the line should be at least 7 lb (3.2 kg) breaking strain, otherwise a clean break can be expected. Never give a chub slack line, for it rapidly takes advantage of this and snags you, and do not expect two fish from one small hole; just be grateful if you land one and then move on to the next chub haunt.

Dace

The dace is an extremely active fish, and is constantly on the move, darting rapidly from one position to another as it picks up food particles.

In colour the fish is basically silver, the back varying from darkish green to a brown hue depending on the water in which it lives. The fins are tinted with yellow or pale pink, while the caudal (tail fin) often shows little coloration. Many anglers have great difficulty in spotting the difference between small chub and specimen dace. The most practical method of defining the two species is by the shape of the dorsal and anal fins (see Fig. 24). The fins of the dace are concave, whilst those of the chub are convex. Chub also give the appearance of being a much coarser fish, as the scales are larger and the head and mouth are heavier than those of a dace of corresponding size.

The average size of dace caught by anglers is usually 2 or 3 oz (0.028–0.056 kg) and anything over ½ lb (0.22 kg) is considered a good fish. Dace, however, will grow larger and the record now stands at 1 lb 8 oz 5 drams (c.68 kg), and was taken from a side stream of the Hampshire Avon.

Feeding habits

Dace are mainly surface or mid-water feeders, taking much of their food in insect form. On certain occasions they will feed close to the bottom, but this occurs mainly in the winter months, or if they are disturbed by rivercraft, etc.

Baits

There are very few baits that dace will not, at some time or another, accept and any of the following will catch fish on most occasions: maggots, worms (all types catch dace) and silkweed – this is the soft weed that grows on weirs and locks, etc. To bait up with silkweed the hook should be dragged across a patch until the hook is suitably adorned. Bread is also taken in various forms; such as crust, flake and paste. Hempseed is an excellent dace bait, as are elderberries. It often pays to groundbait with hemp and fish with a ripe elderberry on your hook.

(Fig. 24)

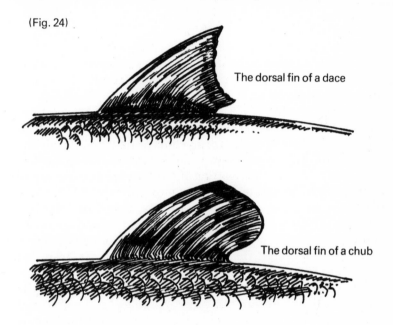

The dorsal fin of a dace

The dorsal fin of a chub

Groundbaits

Dace respond well to groundbait and I find that a bait with a base of stale bread to be a good one. If maggots are to be the hook bait, a few should be included each time a ball of groundbait is thrown out.

Location

Dace are found in a great number of waters in both England and Wales, but not in Scotland. They are to be found in only one Irish river. These fast-moving fish normally prefer fast, well aerated water, although I have caught fine dace from a slow-moving canal. In the warmer months, dace will congregate in shallower swims, especially if weed grows in these places, while winter dace will drop back into deeper water, although, once again, I have occasionally had good sport from swims of less than four feet (1.22 m) in depth. Once the floods start, dace move out of the full force of the current and feed in sheltered spots.

Tackle

Rods

There is no need to have a separate outfit for dace as normal roach tackle will be sufficient. A match rod with fast action is the one to use when trying to contact fast-biting dace.

Hooks

These should be small, size 14 or 16 for float work, and 10 or 12 when legering.

Floats

Porcupine or bird quills are the most useful for dace floats although, occasionally, a quill with a light cork or balsa body may be necessary, especially if the current happens to be faster than normal.

Methods

Float fishing

A dace will take and eject a bait very rapidly, and often the float will merely flicker and then resume its steady course down the swim. At first the angler's reactions will be too slow, but as the day advances they should become faster and the angler should eventually be hooking one in every three fish that take the bait. I have noticed, however, that the smaller the dace the faster the bite, so, if I suspect that larger specimens are present in the swim, I wait for a better bite.

Big dace normally cause the float to tremble, and then they quickly give a substantial pull. It is wise to regard the first tremble as a warning and prepare for the better bite. Dace are extremely wary, so when one fish is hooked it should be hustled rapidly out of the swim and not allowed to splash on the surface, or the rest of the shoal will scatter and may not feed again that day.

The size of the bait depends upon the type of water to be fished, although it always pays to use a slightly larger bait where the current is strong and a smaller bait where it is weak. I decide the depth when I first start to fish a swim by using a plummet, then fish the bait close to the river bed. If nothing happens after half a dozen casts I slide the float down the line so that the bait is, say, 12 in (0.3 m) from the bottom. I keep repeating this until I find fish or decide that dace are not present in the chosen swim. Sometimes fish that have been feeding will suddenly go right off, at which point I alter depth until I find their new feeding level. This sudden change may happen a dozen times during the course of a day but, as a rule, it only means that the fish have moved to a different depth. When the float arrives at the end of the swim it should be held back so that the bait precedes it and then rises invitingly up from its original course (see Fig. 25). Large dace seem to find this manoeuvre fascinating and it often accounts for the biggest fish of the day.

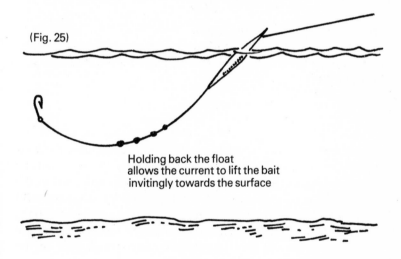

(Fig. 25)

Holding back the float
allows the current to lift the bait
invitingly towards the surface

Legering

Legering often produces better quality fish than float fishing and it pays to use a slightly larger bait. My favourite all-round bait when legering for dace is a large redworm, although maggots work well and in extremely cold weather I have caught many fish on breadpaste and crust.

63

This very efficient method was originated, I believe, on the Thames and the Kennet. To fish this method properly, a deepish swim close to the bank must be found where the current does not run too fast. In fact, the slower the water the better. The depth of water must first be found and then the float set some 15 in (40 cm) deeper than the depth of the actual swim. Groundbait is then thrown in, followed by the baited tackle which is allowed to trot down for 4 or 5 yards (3.6 or 4.5 m) and is then held back whilst the current causes the bait to rise up from the bottom. If no bite is forthcoming the float should be worked a few paces downstream and the process repeated. Dace usually find this method enticing and their bites are decisive affairs that are easy to strike at.

Fly fishing

The best fly rod is invariably one built of carbon fibre; unfortunately, these are extremely expensive. A good substitute is a hollow fibreglass rod. The length, of course, depends on the water to be fished. If it is open, a long rod will be needed; a shorter one, if the water is heavily overhung with trees and brambles. For all-round use, I find 8½ ft (2.5 m) to be best.

Any medium-sized fly reel can be used for dace fishing. I use and like an Intrepid rimfly reel.

Fly line is always an expensive item, so it is much the best bet to buy a good one to start with. Although, by looking carefully through the various advertisements in fly-fishing magazines it *is* possible to purchase slightly sub-standard fly lines at a fraction of the normal cost of a perfect line and these lines are ideal for dace fishing. For easy casting, a line with a forward taper (see Fig. 26) will give the best results. Dace are surface feeders, consequently a floating line should be used to place the fly on or just beneath the surface as a sinking line would pull the fly below the normal feeding level of the dace shoals.

For all forms of fly fishing the nylon cast should be tapered, so that the thick end is joined to the reel line while the thin end is attached to the fly. These casts can be bought or else made up at home from various lengths of nylon. A perfectly usable cast can also be made from a single length of 2 or 3 lb (0.9–1.4 kg) bs nylon. Purists will argue that a tapered cast enables the fly to be presented perfectly. I have my doubts and find I catch just as many fish with a cast cut directly from a spool of nylon.

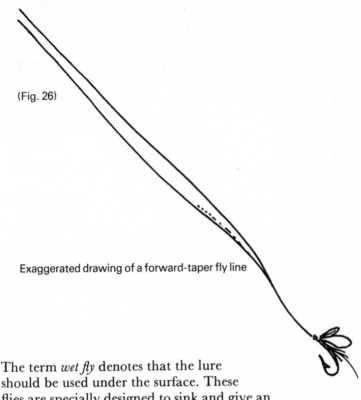

(Fig. 26)

Exaggerated drawing of a forward-taper fly line

The term *wet fly* denotes that the lure should be used under the surface. These flies are specially designed to sink and give an appearance of lifelike movement when worked by the angler. The wings and hackles of wet flies (see Fig. 27) point back, down the shank of the hook. This helps to give the fly its lifelike appearance.

(Fig. 27)

A typical wet fly has its wings and hackles pointing backwards

A *dry fly* is designed to float and should correspond, where possible, to the natural insect upon which the fish are feeding. On dry flies the hackles are stiff and more upright than on wet flies and this helps the lure to float.

It is well to remember that dace prefer a small fly, so hook sizes should be oo down to 1 (fly scale). I seldom carry more than half a dozen patterns, namely Coachman, Greenwell's Glory, Olive Dun, Coch-y-bondhu, Alder and Olive Quill. These can be obtained in either wet or dry patterns, and three or four of each should last out the season.

Eels

The eel is a mysterious creature which spends the bulk of its life in fresh water, but is born and dies in the sea. All the small eels that reach our shore and ascend our rivers start life in the weedy depths of the Sargasso Sea; and after reaching maturity most of them begin the return journey to breed.

During the early part of the year enormous numbers of young eels (elvers) make their way into rivers and streams to begin their lives in inland waters. Nothing seems to stop elvers from reaching their objective, and folk lore has it that they even take to the land in an attempt to reach waters which are cut off from inlet or outlet streams.

The eel record is held by a fish weighing 11 lb 2 oz (5.05 kg) caught in 1978 from Kingfisher Lake in Hampshire. Larger eels are known to exist and with the ever-increasing interest in big-eel fishing it can only be a matter of time before eels in excess of the present record are taken. Big eels are by no means common, however, although there are probably more of them about than most anglers realise. No one really knows just what weight a big eel can attain, but there is strong evidence to show that eels weighing up to at least 15 lb (6.8 kg) exist in British waters. Big eels are probably hooked fairly frequently by anglers using worm or fish baits, but owing to their strength the eels usually break free long before they can be brought to the surface and the breakages are usually put down to carp or pike. Small eels are prolific, particularly in waters situated within a few miles of the sea. These immature specimens often make a nuisance of themselves as they will attack almost any natural bait, usually managing to swallow the hook in the process.

Because of this many anglers have a hatred of all eels, which is a pity as big eels are wonderful fighting fish and have none of the unpleasant habits of their smaller brethren.

Feeding habits

Eels are predatory fish, which eat almost any small creature, live or dead, which comes their way. They are especially fond of the spawn of other species.

Baits

The lists of baits which can be used successfully for eel fishing is a lengthy one, and includes frogs, offal, liver and swan mussels, as well as the more normal worms, maggots and fish baits. Blood is a great eel attractant and some specimen hunters use a hypodermic syringe to pump deadbaits full of ox blood before using them. The eel is also a cannibal and will eat small eels whole as well as portions of cut-up eel. Large lobworms or garden worms are best used whole or even in big bunches. Fresh dead fish is another fine bait.

The ideal size for a deadbait is 4–6 in (10–15 cm), although larger fish can be used when fishing waters known to contain very big eels.

Few eel anglers use livebaits, which is strange as a large eel is an active hunter and will readily accept a livebait. Slim, narrow-bodied fish make the best live or deadbaits because their narrowness allows the eel to take and swallow them quickly.

Location

Large eels can turn up in the most unexpected places. A tiny duckpond, a disused fire tank, even the Serpentine in London's Hyde Park have all produced eels of over 5 lb (2.3 kg) in weight, and because of this almost any water is worth trying for eels. Man-made lakes and pits are good venues as eels seem to thrive in still water and the deep clean water of a pit, particularly a pit which has been disused for a number of years, can produce really large eels. Gravel pits are often fed by streams which give eels easy access to the water and these landlocked waters are one of the best places to seek eel of record-breaking size; for an eel which has succeeded in reaching these waters as an elver is often unable to leave again and this enforced captivity deprives the eel of its opportunity to make the spawning migration; consequently it remains behind, growing ever larger and larger as the years pass.

In waters which contain only stunted fish, eel fishing gives anglers their best opportunity of catching a fish of specimen size, and this alone should be enough to encourage people to persevere with eel hunting, for a 3–5 lb (1.4–2.3 kg) eel provides more sport and excitement than a netful of tiny roach, perch or rudd. After all, eels can thrive and put on weight in waters in which other types of fish have to struggle to find enough food to keep them alive; for the eel is an active hunter and small fish form a major part of its food chain.

Choosing an eel swim

Almost any section of a given water is capable of producing eels, although most anglers prefer to fish the deepest holes. It does not pay to overcast when eel hunting, for most of the fish will live close to the bank, in holes or among sunken tree roots. Big eels seem to have definite territories which are usually within easy reach of their retreats. Once hooked they immediately make a determined effort to swim under some nearby obstruction. Shallow water should not be ignored where eels are concerned, as big eels often venture into the shallows in search of food. When a stiff wind has ruffled the water's surface and stirred up mud and silt in the shallows, eels of all sizes sometimes move into water only a few inches in depth. At these times worms make the best bait, for the eels become preoccupied with small natural bait to such an extent that they ignore dead fishbait completely.

The eel is a summer species which goes into semi-hibernation during the colder months. It is also a nocturnal creature and night fishing is essential if eels are to be caught consistently. As not everyone wishes to stay up all night, it is fortunate that one of the best times to find eels feeding is from twilight to approximately two hours after dark. Water temperature plays a most important part in eel fishing and the higher the temperature, the better the chance of sport. Daylight eel fishing is at best an uncertain occupation, for eels usually remain in their holes during full daylight and even if they do emerge to feed, they keep well away from the bank. A freshly-caught deadbait is the best bait for daytime eel fishing. Daylight eel fishing is a slow business, but it is a good way of passing a hot day and will occasionally yield an eel of specimen size.

Tackle

Normal coarse-fishing tackle is useless for big-eel fishing and any angler who has the misfortune to hook an eel of specimen size on a light outfit will have the kit broken up in the first few minutes of battle.

Rods

A heavy-duty pike or carp rod is the ideal as it has both the length and the strength to successfully subdue a large eel.

Reels

A medium size fixed-spool reel is the most popular for modern eel fishing.

Lines

A 10 lb (4.5 kg) breaking strain is the minimum strength of line to use and even this may be a little light for use in weedy water, so it is advisable to carry a spare reel spool filled with 12 or even 15 lb (5.4–6.8 kg) bs line.

Hooks

There was a time when any cheap hook was referred to as an eel hook. Fortunately times have changed and eel anglers now realise the importance of using the best and most reliable hooks obtainable; for no matter how good the remainder of the tackle might be, the hook is still the direct link between angler and eel, and badly tempered hooks can only lead to lost fish. There are now many robust and well-designed specimen hooks on the market. Hook sizes 2 and 4 are the most useful, but if big deadbait is used a size 1–0 hook can be employed.

Traces

Eels have powerful jaws filled with fine but sharp, small teeth, which can easily sever strong nylon. A wire trace is, therefore, essential for big-eel fishing. Braided wire is better than single-strand wire, which has a tendency to kink in use and snap under pressure. Polyester fibre (Dacron) can also be used instead of wire and has the advantage of being both soft and supple.

Further thoughts on tackle

All the tackle described here may appear heavy to the novice eel angler, but a big eel is not a fish to be taken lightly. A 5 lb (2.3 kg) eel will fight as hard as a 10 lb (4.5 kg) pike or carp and there is always the chance that an eel of record size will find and take the bait.

Landing

A deep fine-meshed landing net is undoubtedly the most effective instrument to use for landing eels. Hexagon-mesh landing nets are ideal for eel fishing.

Methods

A plain running leger is the best terminal tackle to use for deadbait fishing, the length of trace being immaterial. Extra weight in the form of a swivelled lead can be added, if necessary, but weight should be kept to the absolute minimum as big eels are wary fish and will drop a bait if they feel the added drag of a large lead. Under normal circumstances the weight of the deadbait is adequate for casting purposes.

Deadbaits

The simplest and most successful method of mounting a deadbait is to thread it directly on to the trace with a baiting needle. As the diagram shows, the trace is passed through the vent of the bait and out of its mouth. The hook is then tied to the trace and pulled back so that the bend and point of the hook project from the mouth of the bait (see Fig. 28). Eels, like all predators, swallow a bait head first, and mounting the bait so that the hook is in the head end ensures that, when the strike is made, the hook will be well inside the eel's mouth. A stop shot should be clipped on to the trace, close to the vent of the bait. This serves a dual purpose. Firstly, it stops the bait from sliding back up the line and, secondly it stops a hooked eel from blowing the bait away from its jaws. This is important for a fairly nasty reason, for if the bait stays in place it serves to gag the eel, which in turn makes it difficult for the eel to breathe and fight properly, not

(Fig. 28)

swivel

A deadbait mounted for eel fishing,
with the bend and barb projecting from its mouth

very sporting but then eel hunting is a rough game with few rules. Fresh baits are essential, for, contrary to popular belief, eels are clean feeders. Remember, however, to make sure that the bait's air bladder is broken before casting out, otherwise the deadbait will float up instead of settling down on to the bottom in a natural manner. The simplest way of breaking the air bladder is to crush the bait underfoot; this not only breaks the bladder but also damages the bait so that its body juices wash out in the water to create a lane of smell that helps to attract hungry eels.

Livebaits

Eels take livebaits intended for pike and perch and yet, strangely enough, few anglers deliberately fish with livebaits for eels. There is, however, an ever-increasing interest in this branch of eel fishing and a number of specimen hunters are carrying out detailed research on the problems and possibilities of livebait fishing for big eels. A leger is still the most popular technique to use. This varies only slightly from the leger described in the deadbait section, except that a lead of some sort must be used, for a livebait on a free line will quickly entangle the line in some obstruction. A livebait tethered by a weight will simply swim about in a confined area, the extent of this area being determined by the length of trace that is used. Livebaits should be hooked through the top lip.

Timing the strike

Big eels take bait in a similar way to pike, consequently the strike should be delayed until the eel has had ample time to turn and swallow the bait. Premature strikes lead to lost fish.

Eels are often hooked well inside the mouth or throat, and this can make the removal of the hook a tricky operation. Because of this, eel anglers often prefer to cut the line close to the eel's mouth and sacrifice the hook. Of course, if the fish is to be kept for eating then the hook can be removed at home, but most eel anglers prefer to return their catches alive to the water, complete with hook. The eel is a tough creature and will soon rid itself of the hook and short length of line.

Grayling

The grayling is a beautiful and graceful fish, well worth the angler's attention. Basically a silvery blue, it has a greenish tint to the head and back. The anal and caudal fins usually have a faint tinge of red, as does the large well-shaped dorsal fin. Correctly speaking, the grayling is a member of the salmon family, as can be seen by the tiny adipose fin set between the dorsal and tail, but in general appearance it resembles a coarse fish in having rather roach-like scales.

Grayling have a number of nicknames, the most suitable and pleasant being 'the Lady of the Stream', 'the Queen' and 'Flower of the River'.

Feeding habits

Grayling will eat all types of insect and they also take vegetable matter, probably to extract minute water life from it.

Baits

Worms and maggots are the best grayling baits, but occasionally grayling will accept bread. As this species rises readily to insects that fall to the surface, it offers great opportunities to the fly fisherman. The grayling will take both wet and dry flies, provided it is not disturbed by bad casting.

Location

Originally a fish from the North of the British Isles, the grayling has been introduced to a number of Southern chalk streams where it has thrived and multiplied in the fast clean water. Unfortunately, many trout fishermen object to the grayling on the grounds that it deprives the trout of a great deal of food and, consequently, vast numbers of grayling are caught and killed each season. This policy is leading to the utter destruction of one of our most beautiful species, which is a sad state of affairs.

Tackle

Rods

For trotting down a normal trotting rod is ideal. For fly casting a special fly rod and tackle must be used and this is described in the Trout chapter.

Reels

Provided the line runs freely from the reel, it is immaterial whether it is a centre-pin or fixed-spool type.

Lines

Nylon of 3 lb (1.4 kg) breaking strain is sufficient and on clear weedless water this can be reduced to $2\frac{1}{2}$ lb (1.1 kg).

Floats

The most popular float when fishing for grayling is the Avon-style trotting float.

Hooks

For all-round use, hook sizes 10, 12 and 14 are excellent. Grayling have smallish mouths and a big hook is a disadvantage. Sometimes, when the fish are very shy, it is sensible to change over to a size 18 or 20, baited with a single maggot.

Methods

During the summer months grayling tend to keep out of the main current and feed in slacker water (see Fig. 29). This habit can be very useful, as it enables the angler to stand well upstream and let the bait run down with the current, so that the bait gradually works out of the main sweep of the river and into the quieter water, bringing the food naturally into the view of the waiting fish.

(Fig. 29)

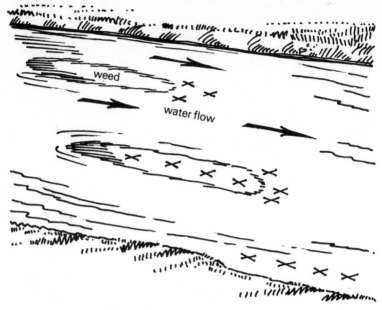

weed

water flow

During the summer, fish such as grayling feed just out of the main current

Bites usually occur the instant the bait enters the slack area and are easy to strike at. Once a fish is hooked, hustle it out into the main river so that the rest of the shoal are not disturbed. In this manner it is often possible to extract a number of fish from one swim.

I usually fish the bait 1–2 in (2½–5 cm) from the river bed but sometimes the grayling rise to mid-water, especially if the day happens to be warm and sunny, so always experiment until the feeding level is found.

It is not necessary to carry a great deal of tackle when grayling fishing for it is a roving occupation and may well lead you up or down river for about 2–3 miles/kilometres in the course of a day.

Winter grayling

Grayling will still feed during periods of intense cold but rather spasmodically and it is worth spending more time at each pool. Do not groundbait heavily when fishing in winter, instead throw in half a dozen maggots every nine or ten casts.

Winter grayling also prefer a smaller bait and a single maggot or tiny redworm will be sufficient. Bites are less decisive and may only cause the float to move a little to the right or left of its normal path. At all times be prepared to strike, for even a slight delay will give the fish time to eject the bait.

Fly casting

Grayling are free and easy risers and will happily accept a dry fly. Favourite patterns are either Red Ant or Greenwells Glory. Wet flies will also produce fish and a Coachman seems to be a reliable pattern.

Nymphs also seem to fascinate the grayling and in the deeper pools a leaded nymph is excellent.

Perch

The dividing line between small- or medium-sized perch and big perch is a very distinct one; for once these fish attain a weight of over 2 lb (0.9 kg) they change their feeding habits and haunts considerably. Small perch are extremely easy to catch and, on many waters, make a complete and utter nuisance of themselves by gorging down baits intended for other fish. Large perch, on the other hand, are extremely difficult to locate and even more difficult to catch. In consequence there are few anglers in this country who can claim to have taken perch of over 4 lb (1.8 kg) in weight, and even fish in the 3 lb–4 lb (1.4–1.8 kg) range are far from common.

I must admit that I find perch extremely interesting and whenever the opportunity arises to fish a water that is known to contain perch of specimen size, I arrive at the venue at the earliest possible hour and don't pack up my rods until well after dusk.

I usually manage to catch a few specimens during the course of a season, and although I have yet to land a perch of over 4 lb (1.8 kg), I feel that it is only a matter of time before I achieve this ambition. On at least three separate occasions I have hooked, seen and ultimately lost perch which at a conservative estimate would have easily topped the 4 lb (1.8 kg) mark. This business of hooking and losing big perch is a problem which confronts every dedicated perch angler, for the mouth and lips of a perch are very delicate and often the hook will only penetrate the thin membrane that joins the lips to the face of the fish. This membrane tears very easily under pressure and once this has happened, the chances are that the hook will simply drop out before the perch can be brought within range of the landing net. The only way to counteract this problem is to play the fish on as tight a line as possible.

Feeding habits

The perch is a predator which will generally hide in reeds and rushes to ambush smaller fish and other creatures as they come within striking distance. Although, at certain times of the year, perch will group to feed on fry and minnows.

Baits

Large lobworms account for the majority of the big perch caught in this country. Livebaits work equally well but are difficult to cast any distance. Gudgeon have always been regarded as the best livebait for perch fishing, but I would say that they are definitely inferior to 'shiny' fish, such as roach, dace and bleak. Bleak are, in fact, my favourite livebait and, although legend has it that the bleak is an extremely frail, delicate little fish which dies very easily when used for bait, I have always found it to be the exact reverse, and on many occasions I have known a bleak to outlast roach and dace baits.

Many perch anglers still use tiny livebaits and discard anything over 3 or 4 in ($7\frac{1}{2}$ or 10 cm) in length as being too big. This is nonsense, particularly if you intend to fish for very big perch. Wherever possible I use bait between 6–7 in (15–$17\frac{1}{2}$ cm) long, for I have found in the past that on average small baits produce small fish. There are, of course, exceptions to this rule but these are few and far between. Consequently I find it better to employ a big bait and then wait for a better quality fish.

Worms, of course, have always been first-class perch bait. Unfortunately they also produce a great many smallish perch but, even so, it always pays to carry a tin of large lobworms just in case other baits are unobtainable.

Deadbaits

In recent years deadbaiting has become a recognised perch technique, and many big fish have fallen to large deadbaits fished on leger tackle. Top Norfolk angler, John Wilson, takes many of his best perch on small dead perch. I have tried deadbaits on a number of occasions and have caught perch to 2 lb

10 oz (1.2 kg). Deadbaiting is, however, a slow method of fishing and unless you are prepared to spend a considerable length of time waiting for a 'run' to develop, my advice is to stick to the more conventional techniques. It is extremely interesting to note that all predatory or semi-predatory fish will take deadbaits with confidence. During 1980-1981 some huge chub were taken on baited whole dead mackerel (see Chub chapter).

Artificial baits

Perch, particularly the medium-sized fish, are greatly attracted by the flash and glitter of an artificial lure, and for the angler interested in sport alone, a good bag of fish and great fun can be had from a day's spinning with ultra-light tackle on a reasonably productive perch water. However, spinning is seldom practised by anglers interested in catching very big perch for, although the odd outsized fish does succumb to the attractive sparkle of some well-finished spoon or plug bait, in general artificial baits do not seem to appeal to the really large fish. Even so, I occasionally spend a happy day, armed only with a rod, reel and landing net, spinning for perch and I must admit I enjoy these outings immensely. Perch are not fussy about artificial lures nor do they have an attraction to a particular colour. If the perch are in a feeding mood, then they will hit just about any artificial lure irrespective of its colour scheme!

Location

For some inexplicable reason perch waters run in distinct cycles. For a comparatively short while they will fish extremely well, producing large perch consistently. After this they go right 'off' and both the numbers and the quality of the fish landed gradually decrease until the big fish appear to become extinct, leaving behind only hordes of minute perch fry which commit suicide in their traditional manner by swallowing each and every worm-baited or maggot-baited hook that comes their way.

It is interesting to note that, as the number of big perch in a water decreases, so other species come to the fore. In one water I know, the fish that came in were carp, while in another water, roach became the predominant species. There is little doubt, in my mind anyway, that there are far more large perch about than most anglers realise: this is particularly true of gravel pits,

1 A double-figure barbel from the River Wensum, Norfolk *(top)*.

2 Barbel anglers on the Avon at Christchurch, Dorset *(right)*.

All photographs by Trevor Housby except nos. 1, 7, 15, 23, 37 and 49 (J. Wilson).

3   Peter Ellery with an 8 lb 2 oz (3.68 kg) bream from Broadlands lake, Hampshire *(top left)*.

4   Five bream to 10¼ lb (4.65 kg), Hatchet pond, New Forest *(top right)*.

5   A nice common bream *(left)*.

6   Fishing for bream, Hatchet pond *(right)*.

7   Head of specimen common bream *(right, inset)*.

8   Author with a brace of wild carp *(top left)*.

9   A fine Hampshire crucian carp *(top right)*.

10 A 21 lb (9.5 kg) mirror carp *(far left)*.

11 A typical crucian carp water, Paradise pool, Hampshire *(centre left)*.

12 Returning a 19 lb (8.6 kg) mirror carp *(left)*.

13 Unhooking an Avon chub *(top left)*.

14 A near-record golden orfe from Broadlands lake *(left)*.

15 John Wilson with a chub and a roach *(right)*.

16 A nice dace caught on a Grice & Young centre-pin reel *(left)*.

17 Netting a River Test grayling *(top left)*.

18 A 2 lb (0.9 kg) grayling safely netted *(top right)*.

19 A brown trout and grayling on fly *(above)*.

20 The head of a 2 lb 2 oz (0.96 kg) grayling *(top left)*.

21 A perch from a Norfolk broad *(top right)*.

22 Specimen grayling for a lady angler *(bottom far left)*.

23 Three nice grayling on dry fly *(bottom left)*.

24 A typical perch *(above left)*.

25 A nice bright perch in perfect condition *(above right)*.

26 A 12 lb (5.4 kg) pike
   spinner *(left)*.

27 Netting a near 20 lb
   (9 kg) pike *(centre top)*

28 Note the superb shape
   of this pike *(centre
   bottom)*.

29 Big pike on a plug bai
   (top right).

30 Author with 18 lb (8.2
   kg) pike *(bottom right*

31 A 26 lb 2 oz (11.85 kg
   pike from Broadlands
   lake *(bottom far right*

32 Author with a 26½ lb (12 kg) pike *(left)*.

33 Winter roach angler *(top)*.

34 Netting a roach *(bottom left)*.

35 Returning a Hampshire Avon roach *(bottom right)*.

36 An average rudd *(top left)*.

37 A specimen rudd *(left)*.

38 Playing a good fish, Hatchet pond *(right)*.

39 A 5 lb (2.25 kg) tench *(right, inset)*.

40 A brace of specimen tench, Broadlands lake *(top left)*.

41 Dry fly water—upper Test *(top right)*.

42 Author with a fine tench *(bottom right)*.

43 Fly fishing Leominstead lake, Lyndhurst *(bottom far right)*.

44 A fine brown trout from the River
   Test *(top left)*.

45 Author with a brace of rainbow
   trout *(left)*.

46 Head of a giant rainbow trout
   caught by Trevor Housby *(right)*.

47 A brace of beautifully marked brown trout caught on nymph *(top left)*.

48 Brook trout caught from a Hampshire lake *(left)*.

49 Zander, note the use of a small bait, in this case a gudgeon *(right)*.

50 Waiting for a bite, Hatchet pond *(overleaf)*.

for often these man-made lakes are so large and so deep that it is difficult to fish more than a fraction of the area. Perch stocks in this country have, unfortunately, suffered heavy losses from disease during the past decade and this disease has wiped out perch stocks in many areas. There are, however, signs that perch are staging a comeback.

Tackle

The perch is not a particularly dashing fighter. Although many angling writers in the past have portrayed the perch as a gallant and very strong creature, it is only necessary to look at the tail of the fish, which is tiny in comparison with its thick hump-backed body, to see that although the perch has all the spirit in the world it is physically incapable of putting up much of a fight when hooked. Even a big perch can be handled on light tackle providing, of course, it does not manage to sidle under or round some underwater obstruction.

Bearing in mind that the perch is incapable of fighting to any great extent, it should be possible to catch these handsome fish on ultra-light tackle. Unfortunately, long casting techniques are often required to drop the bait on to the known feeding grounds and, as this calls for the use of a lead weighing $\frac{3}{4}$ oz (0.02 kg) or more, a reasonably substantial line and rod have to be used.

Rods

The rods I employ are Mk IV Avons used in conjunction with fixed-spool reels and a line of 6 lb (2.7 kg) breaking strain. The Avon-type rods are quite suitable for all aspects of perch fishing.

Hooks

At various times I have tried a wide variety of hooks for perch fishing. Trebles I have long since discarded for, although they have great hooking power, they can damage a fish very badly. This I dislike intensely for, whenever possible, I like to return the fish I catch alive and unharmed to the water. Double salmon-fly hooks, on the other hand, I have used with great success, particularly when using a livebait on leger tackle (see Fig. 30). Apart from this, I have always found a size 2 or 4 round-bend hook to be perfectly satisfactory.

(Fig. 30)

A double salmon-fly hook is very useful when livebaiting for perch

Setting up the rods

Big perch are extremely cautious fish. At the slightest check to their movements they will eject a suspect bait and depart in panic to a safer area. For this reason great care should be taken when setting up the rods. Two rod-rests for each rod are a must and any projecting grass or weed should be cleared away or else covered up between these rests, otherwise the bite indicator may catch up as a taking fish pulls line from the reel spool. A good plan is to lay a small groundsheet on top of the grass; then it will be almost impossible for the moving line to catch up. For perch fishing the lightest possible indicator should be employed. A piece of silver paper folded over the line (see Fig. 31) is quite adequate. A taking perch will usually make a long initial run. Consequently, it is necessary to open the pick-up of the reel and also to make absolutely certain that the line can run freely through the silver paper indicator and not jam up in any way. Silver paper indicators work extremely well provided that there is little or no wind.

(Fig. 31)

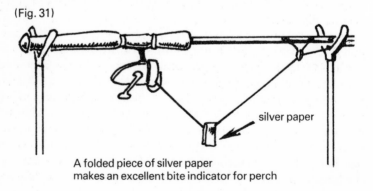

silver paper

A folded piece of silver paper
makes an excellent bite indicator for perch

If, however, there is even a moderate wind the paper will tend to blow from side to side and this can be annoying, as the swaying movement will cause a few coils of loose line to slip off the reel and this may result in a nasty tangle. To overcome this possibility a matchstick can be attached to the rod butt by means of an elastic band (see Fig. 32) and the line can be clipped lightly under the matchstick. This will beat the wind but at the same time the slightest pull from a hungry perch will free the line, allowing it to run out freely.

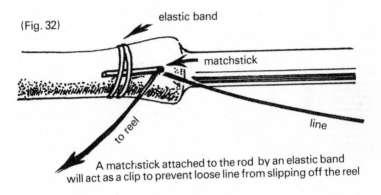

(Fig. 32)

elastic band

matchstick

to reel

line

A matchstick attached to the rod by an elastic band will act as a clip to prevent loose line from slipping off the reel

Methods

Float fishing

I have always looked upon float fishing for perch as a summer technique, and as a rule I discard it in favour of the leger with the onset of winter, mainly, I suppose, because I feel that during the early part of the season when the water temperature is consistently high the perch will often swim and feed within easy casting distance of the bank. Later on, when water temperatures start to decrease, the perch forsake their summer haunts and retire to the deeper areas well away from the shore.

Float tackle for perch fishing need not be elaborate. Provided that the float supports the bait satisfactorily, that is all that matters. Normally, I set the float so that the bait is suspended at about 1 ft (30 cm) off the bottom. Very occasionally, if I happen to notice a perch actively chasing small fry close to the surface, I will reel in and adjust the float so that the bait hangs just beneath the surface but normally I prefer to fish close to the bottom, for that is where I expect the perch to feed. During the summer months, when there are plenty of small fish about, it is possible to attract large perch to your baited tackle by throwing out groundbait. This does not interest the perch, but it does attract hordes of small fry, and these in turn bring in the perch. On gravel pits that are still being worked it often pays to fish in the vicinity of the dredgers or mechanical scoops, as perch are often attracted by disturbed and muddied water. Under these circumstances worms make the best baits for, after all, when you think about it logically, it is obvious that a great many worms and grubs will be uncovered by the digging operations and many of these will find their way into the water where the perch will be waiting for an easy meal.

Legering

Long-range legering has probably accounted for more big perch than any other method devised. For leger fishing with a worm bait, the length of 'trace' between hook and lead can range from 12-24 in (30-60 cm), sometimes even more, but if you intend to use a legered livebait I suggest that the distance between hook and lead should be increased to between 4-5 ft (1.2-1.5 m). This will make casting rather difficult, but if you can manage to overcome this problem you will find that your catches will increase accordingly.

On one water I fish, it is most unusual to get a run on short-trace tackle. On several occasions I have set up two rods, one made up so that the bait was within 5 ft (1.5 m) of the lead and the other set so that the livebait had 3 ft (0.9 m) between it and the lead. For every fish I caught on the short-trace rig, I took four with the other tackle. Frankly, I don't think it is the lead that puts the perch off. Indeed, I am sure that before the perch will take the livebait it will chase it about for a while.

On the long trace the livebait has more scope to move, and this movement probably excites and infuriates the hunting perch to such an extent that it takes the bait in a firm and decisive fashion before the bait has a chance to escape.

On the shorter link-tackle the livebait has little chance to skip about and in consequence the attacking perch may become suspicious and refuse to take the bait. This theory is backed up by the antics of the silver paper bite indicator on the short trace rod, which often lifts, trembles and twitches indicating that the livebait is alarmed. Seldom, however, do these movements develop into a full-blooded run. Occasionally, when I have wound the tackle in after a bout of 'twitches' on the indicator, I have found the livebait to be dead, often with large patches of scales missing from its back and sides. I think, in these cases, that small perch were responsible as, on several occasions, I have watched three or four perch in the 6 to 8 in (15-20 cm) class harrying roach or rudd almost as big as themselves. Obviously perch of this size are unable to swallow the other fish, but their hunting instincts are so strong that they attack regardless of the large size of their quarry. Usually when a perch takes a legered livebait the bite will follow a distinct pattern. First the indicator will rise smoothly as far as the first rod ring, then the line will start to stream out at a steady speed. As a rule I wait until the running fish has taken 8 to 10 yards (7.3-9.1 m) of line, then I engage the pick-up of the reel and strike the instant I feel the movement of the taking fish against the rod tip. When I started perch fishing I used to strike at the first indication of a run, but I lost so many fish because of this that I learnt to control my reactions and delay the strike until the perch had had sufficient time to turn and swallow the bait.

Drift line fishing

This is a floatless leadless method which can be extremely effective when the perch are feeding close to the bank. The tackle is very simple and the weight of the livebait makes it sufficient for casting purposes. As no float or other indicator is used for this form of fishing, I find that it always pays to hold the rod. At the same time, the line should be watched with great care, and as soon as it begins to move away rapidly or behave in any other suspicious manner you should be prepared to 'feed' line off the reel spool, so that the taking fish will feel no resistance to its movement. I occasionally use this method in the late summer or early autumn and, as a rule, I travel light and rove continuously along the banks in search of fish. Perch lend themselves well to this style of angling, and provided that you do not clutter yourself with too much equipment you can have an extremely pleasant and often productive day's fishing.

Time of year

To my mind perch are an autumn and winter species and from my own angling diary I find that the majority of the specimen perch I or my companions have landed, have mostly been winter-caught fish, quite a number having been taken during January and February. I feel, however, that I have not spent enough time summer fishing for perch as yet to draw any firm conclusions on this subject, and it may well be that a warm-weather perch programme would produce first-class results.

The only drawback to perch fishing in warm weather, as I see it, is the problem of locating fish in the first instance; for when the water temperatures are high, the perch will tend to wander about from one area to another. This, of course, does not occur nearly as much during prolonged periods of cold weather, for then the perch congregate in the deeper holes where, provided that you can drop your baited tackle into one of these spots, chances are that it will land within reach of a fish. Naturally enough, when the fish are grouped in certain areas you stand a far greater chance of success. This is true of both river and still-water perch.

Perch are not a fast-growing species, and a 4 lb (1.8 kg) fish would probably be in excess of eight-years old.

Pike

Pike seem to thrive in the still waters of the gravel-pit/reservoir type. A yearly analysis of the big-pike catches recorded in the angling press, shows that well over 70% of the specimens reported came from gravel pits in various parts of the country. Specimens up to 34 lb (15.5 kg) have been taken during the last season or two and fish weighing 28–32 lb (12.7–13.5 kg) are caught most years. Most of these fish are returned alive and apparently unharmed to the water where, presumably, after a suitable recuperation period, they begin to put on weight again.

There has always been a great deal of controversy over the size of specimen pike, but I am sure that if an average was taken of all the pike caught during the course of a single season, it would show that the average pike in this country weighed 5–8 lb (2.3–3.6 kg). This may sound ridiculous when compared with the weekly winter reports of 20 lb (9 kg) pike but these big fish make news simply because of their size and the number reported in comparison with the number of anglers pike fishing will show that these big pike are very few and far between, even on the most noted of pike waters. Many an expert pike angler has yet to take a specimen above 20 lb (9 kg) in weight, and yet it is common to hear anglers talking of 20 lb (9 kg) pike as though fish of this calibre are an everyday occurrence, which they most definitely are not. Any pike over 10 lb (4.5 kg) can be classed as a good fish, and any pike over 15 lb (6.8 kg) weight as a specimen. It takes just as much skill to catch a 15 lb (6.8 kg) pike as a 20-pounder. It is just the law of averages that for every 20 lb (9 kg) fish there must be a far higher proportion of 15-pounders, and because of this it is more likely that the bait will be taken by a 15-pounder than a 20-pounder.

Every fresh-water angler will be familiar with the outward appearance of the pike. Its long, lean body, huge head and cruel teeth give it a wicked look. Because of this many anglers, who should know better, make a habit of ill-treating any pike they happen to catch. This cruelty is probably motivated by a fear that the fish will bite. This is a pity, for a properly-handled pike is no more dangerous than any other fresh-water fish and should be treated with the respect it deserves.

Match anglers, of course, argue that pike eat all the small fish and generally ruin a fishery. This is far from true. Many of the most productive pike waters support a large number of fine roach, perch, carp and tench, etc, as well as many big pike. It is far more likely that the presence of the pike helps keep the other fish in check, thereby raising the average size of fish caught. Diseased fish also fall easy prey to hungry pike, and this helps to control outbreaks of disease in a water. Pike also eat pike and to some extent keep themselves in check by their cannibalism.

Obviously, in a small water that holds only a limited stock of fish or in a water that is stocked with trout, pike can be a menace but in a normal well-stocked coarse fishery, pike are an asset. Pike also provide the ordinary angler with the opportunity to catch really big fish without undue expense. For this reason alone the pike is well worth conserving.

Feeding habits

Although predatory by nature, the pike is an opportunist who will, at times, eat almost anything that the angler can offer. Normally, however, the pike is a fish-eater. Small pike usually prefer to catch fresh food, but big pike often become scavengers and quite happy to eat any dead fish they come across. Strangely enough, big pike do not even seem to mind overmuch if they eat almost-rotten fish, although I think they are more inclined to go for a fresh dead fish if given the choice.

Baits

As far as I am concerned live fish make the best all-round pike bait, and as pike are not fussy it does not matter really what type of fish you use as bait. Roach, rudd, dace and gudgeon are the most commonly used livebait in this country, mainly because they are easily obtainable in most districts. Small bream also make good pike bait, so do perch.

On several occasions I have used small pike as bait for big pike and found them to be very good fish catchers.

Dead fishbaits are very popular with pike specialists; and there can be little doubt that deadbaits are extremely effective. Deadbait has several advantages over livebait, particularly if the angler concerned dislikes the idea of impaling a live creature on a large hook. Suitable deadbaits can be obtained from the local wet-fish shop. Mackerel, herring, sardine and sprat make the best deadbaits. Why pike accept sea fish as food no-one can really say, but in all probability the pike are attracted by the oily flesh of the bait and, being lazy creatures, are quite content to pick up an easy meal instead of chasing after the shoalfish upon which they normally feed. Most dead-bait-caught pike are big fish and although I have occasionally seen a smallish one caught, the usual run of fish is over 10 lb (4.5 kg) in weight, much higher, on average, than pike caught on livebaits. For the specialist angler this is very important, for by fishing long and hard with deadbaits the small fish can usually be avoided. Trout and grayling also make very good deadbait for pike.

Groundbaiting for pike

There can be little doubt that the judicious use of groundbait in the shape of whole or chopped-up fish definitely does attract pike to a swim. Unfortunately, groundbait of this type not only attracts the fish, it feeds them as well. Because of this, there is a good chance that prowling pike will gorge themselves on the loose baits, and totally disregard a bait which has been carefully mounted on deadbait tackle. The answer is to use a limited number of fish as groundbait, and to make sure that the hooked bait is as large and as fresh as possible.

Location

Under normal circumstances a pike will lurk in a suitably camouflaged place until a shoal of small fish venture close enough for the pike to attack, then it will lunge out and snap up a victim before the shoal has time to scatter. In large lakes, pits and reservoirs, however, pike become rovers and instead of hanging around in one specific area they tend to wander about in search of food. Obviously a man-made water will seldom provide much cover for pike, consequently these fish are forced to hunt far more actively than those in a river or natural lake which has reed beds, tree roots or fallen trees to provide them with shelter.

Tackle

Although big pike rarely put up an impressive battle when hooked, they occasionally make long powerful runs in their attempt to escape and because of this it is essential to use fairly substantial tackle for most forms of pike fishing.

Rods

A light rod, although a delight to use, will not take the strain of casting heavy live- or deadbaits, nor will it have the power necessary to set a largish hook firmly into a bony tooth-filled mouth. A good pike-fishing rod should have a minimum length of 10 ft (3 m). There are now many specially designed pike rods on the market, most of which are 10 or 11 ft (3 or 3.3 m) long and built in two sections. Pike rods are made of fibreglass or carbon fibre. My choice would be for the glass rod. Carbon rods are light but very expensive. For live- or deadbait fishing lightness is of little importance as the rod spends most of its working life supported by rod rests. The ideal all-round pike rod for live-bait and deadbait fishing has a test curve of 2½ lb (1.1 kg) which allows it to be used with lines of 8–16 lb (3.6–7.2 kg) breaking strain.

The rods already mentioned are too heavy for general spinning, for a far lighter rod is necessary to cast light artificial lures any distance. A MKIV carp rod is suitable for general spinning; short rods should definitely be left alone. MKIV has a test curve of approximately 1½ lb (0.7 kg) and is designed for use with lines between 7–12 lb (3.2–5.4 kg) breaking strain. This rod is quite capable of stopping a really heavy pike and yet is light enough to give the utmost sport with medium-sized fish. Recently I caught a large number of pike to 18 lb (8.2 kg) on a tiny 7 ft (2.1 m) plug fishing rod used in conjunction with an Abu 6500 reel. This little rod has provided me with some interesting, informative and highly successful pike fishing.

Reels

Medium-sized or sea-sized fixed-spool reels are best, although for bankside work a large diameter centre-pin can be used.

Multiplying reels are expensive and require a great deal of practice if they are to be used efficiently. A set of spare reel spools should be carried, each loaded with a different breaking strain of line, ranging from 10 lb (4.5 kg) bs up to 16 lb (7.2 kg) breaking strain.

Hooks

Treble hooks are essential for pike fishing, and it is advisable to buy only the best quality hooks as pike are heavy fish and badly-tempered hooks soon give way under the strain of playing a big fish. Many pike anglers use very big treble hooks. This is a mistake, for a big hook is difficult to set whereas a smallish hook will usually penetrate fairly easily. This is important as a pike has a bony mouth.

For livebaiting with medium-sized baits, a size 8 treble hook is large enough, but with big baits and deadbaits, size 4 or 6 trebles should be used. These larger hooks are less likely to tear out of the bait during casting. Single hooks can, of course, be used for pike fishing but are not advisable when big pike are known to be in the water. Always buy loose treble hooks and make up the terminal tackle at home. Traces made up like this, cost less than half the price of made-up traces bought from a tackle shop. Barbless treble hooks are extremely useful for pike fishing. Partridge of Redditch make a special barbless hook. If these are unavailable a standard treble hook can be adapted by flattening the barbs with a pair of pliers. Barbless hooks are both humane and efficient. They penetrate well on the strike and are easily removable once the fish has been netted.

Traces

Pike have long sharp teeth that can easily chafe or cut through ordinary nylon. Because of this it is advisable to use a length of wire between line and hooks. This wire should be attached to the reel line by means of a swivel. There are several types of wire on the market, the best and most supple being braided wire, which is obtainable with or without a nylon covering. Nylon-covered wire is less supple and visually more obvious than braided wire and for this reason the plain wire is better. Trace wire can be bought in 5-25 yard (4.6-22.9 m) coils. A good deal of money can be saved by buying it this way and making up the traces at home. Never continue to use a trace which has become twisted or kinked, for the wire may have become seriously weakened and will probably break under strain.

Floats

There are many specialist pike floats on sale. Choice of float depends on the size of bait. Never use the old fashioned 'Fishing Gazette' type floats, as these offer far too much resistance to a taking fish.

Artificial baits

Artificial lures are legion and many are designed simply to catch the angler rather than the fish. It is wise to choose your lures with great care, making absolutely certain that only the more serviceable patterns are purchased. Bar spoons (see Fig. 33) and large wobbling spoons (see Fig. 34) are both well designed, and can usually be counted on to catch fish. Plugs make good pike baits and will often catch pike when other lures fail. Single- or double-jointed plastic or wooden plugs are best (see Fig. 35).

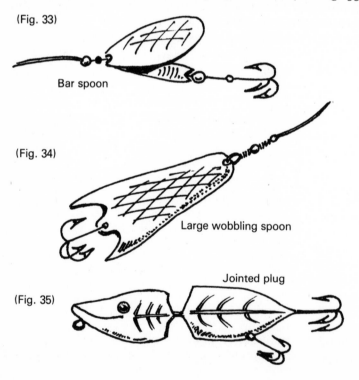

(Fig. 33)

Bar spoon

(Fig. 34)

Large wobbling spoon

Jointed plug

(Fig. 35)

Choice of colour is a matter of personal preference, although I find that the darker patterns are often the best fish catchers. Striped plugs, which look like perch or small pike, are exceptionally good. Light-coloured plugs, on the other hand, seldom seem to arouse the interest of the fish.

Methods

Livebaiting

For livebaiting in deep-water swims close to the bank, or in heavily-weeded swims where a bait fished on standard float tackle would quickly snag up, a float paternoster is the obvious answer. This tackle is easy to cast and provided that it is set up properly in the first place it will anchor the bait firmly in the required spot. Fixed floats are not really suitable for use with paternoster tackle and a streamlined sliding float is essential. A sliding float with a drilled centre-tube is preferable to a float with wire side rings (see Fig. 36), as the side rings tend to cushion the effect of the strike and occasionally catch up in the line during casting. Neither of these problems occurs with a tubed float.

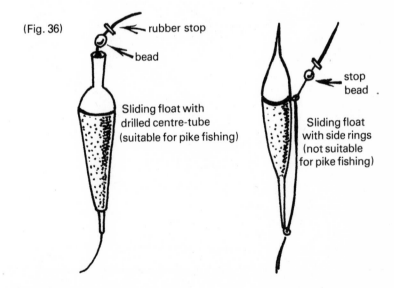

(Fig. 36)

← rubber stop

bead

Sliding float with drilled centre-tube (suitable for pike fishing)

stop bead .

Sliding float with side rings (not suitable for pike fishing)

Although the paternoster looks complicated (see Fig. 37), it is, in fact, extremely simple to set up and use. The line having first

93

been run through the rod rings, a tiny bead or small shirt button should be slid on to the line (see Fig. 38). This will eliminate the possibility of the rubber stop jamming in the top of the float.

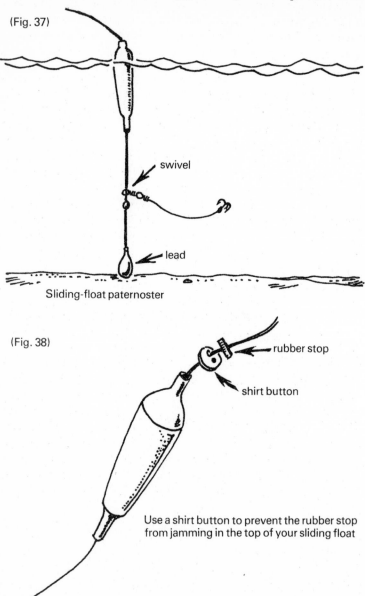

(Fig. 37)

swivel

lead

Sliding-float paternoster

(Fig. 38)

rubber stop

shirt button

Use a shirt button to prevent the rubber stop from jamming in the top of your sliding float

Next, the float can be run on to the line followed by the wire trace. This trace should be attached to a small barrel swivel (see Fig. 39). A three-way swivel can be used, but in practice this type of swivel is inferior to the barrel swivel, for it does not give to the movement of the livebait which results in line twist. The trace should be stopped by a small shot placed approximately 2½ ft (75 cm) up the line. The weight should be knotted to the end of the reel line and a section of rubber band tied to the line above the float. The tackle is then ready for use. The depth of the swim should be carefully ascertained by repeatedly moving the rubber stop up the line until the float cocks just nicely on the surface (see Fig. 40). If the float lies flat or sinks, further adjustment is necessary, but once the float cocks, the stop is correctly positioned and the tackle can be baited and put to work. For paternoster fishing the bait should be liphooked on a treble hook (see Fig. 41). Traces carrying two treble hooks are more nuisance than they are worth on paternoster tackle and have no advantage over traces with one treble hook.

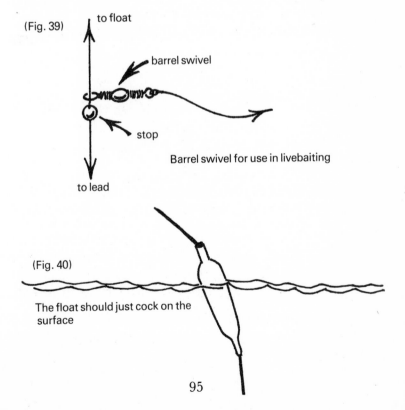

(Fig. 39)

to float

barrel swivel

stop

Barrel swivel for use in livebaiting

to lead

(Fig. 40)

The float should just cock on the surface

95

(Fig. 41)

When fishing for pike
the livebait should be liphooked on one prong of a treble hook

Summer pike fishing

Pike are said to be slow to recover from spawning and for this reason many angling clubs and river boards stipulate that pike fishing must not begin before 1st October. Consequently the majority of anglers regard pike as a winter fish. There is little logic behind this archaic rule, as pike are one of the first fish to spawn and all too often the so-called 'big' end-of-season specimens are gravid female pike on the verge of shedding their spawn. If the weather is particularly mild after Christmas then in all probability pike will spawn during February or early March, at a time when anglers are legally entitled to catch them.

Later, during the summer months, when the fish have fully recovered and are in a fit state to give the best of sport it is illegal in many areas to go pike fishing. Summer pike are often long and lean by comparison to the fat and sleek winter fish but this does not mean they are out of condition or require protection. Far from it, for it is really the bloated spawn-filled winter pike which should be conserved. In a few areas, of course, pike can be fished at any period during the coarse-fishing season, and where this rule applies pike can offer fine sport to the summer angler. As a general rule, pike spend the summer months in shallowish water. It seems amazing that really big pike will live and feed in water barely deep enough to cover their bodies. Pike hooked in the shallows can be relied upon to put up a terrific battle, and will usually fight far harder and longer than a fish of similar size hooked in deep water.

Summer pike seldom have to hunt for food, for the shallows are usually thick with small fry which provide the pike with ample sustenance. Because of this prolific food supply, summer pike have a tendency to become preoccupied with small live fish and will seldom bother to take a deadbait. During the warm months livebait is easy to come by and an hour's fishing with light tackle will usually yield enough small fish for a day's pike fishing. Pike, like most big fish, live in close proximity to weed or reed beds. A bait cast out to fall close to the weeds will often be taken within a few minutes. In shallow water a weight on the line can be a disadvantage and it is advisable to use a weight-less float. Norfolk pike experts use this weightless-float technique to fish the shallow Broads, and the float they use (see Fig. 42) is suitable for fishing all shallow waters. This float can be made up at home by sliding two medium-sized pilot floats on to a suitable length of swan or peacock quill. The pilot floats can be purchased from any fishing-tackle shop. Once again the bait can be liphooked on a treble hook. If the water in the shallows is, for example, 4 ft (1.2 m) in depth, then the float should be set at 2½ ft (75 cm). This will stop the bait from diving to the bottom while still allowing it plenty of room to move about and attract the attention of the pike. As the tackle is weightless, the float will simply lie flat on the surface and will offer little resistance to the bait or to any pike that takes the bait.

(Fig. 42)

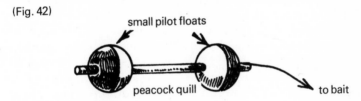

small pilot floats

peacock quill

to bait

Norfolk dumbell for use in shallow water

Shallow-water pike fishing can be a most exciting occupation, for a pike will often leap right out of the shallow water as it takes the bait.

Long-range winter fishing

Pike fishing on really large still-water pits can be extremely frustrating, for the larger pike often lurk in the deepest water well out of casting-range of the bank.

If time is no problem, then it is simply a matter of waiting until one of the big fish ventures in from the deep and takes a bait presented close to the bank. One well-known angler spent a total of 24 days doing just this, and on the last day took a pike of exactly 20 lb (9 kg), a good fish by any standards but was it really worth the length of time spent to catch it? There would have been a greater chance of making contact with a big pike in far less time by getting the bait right out into the really deep water.

Obviously, depositing a bait into an area of water which is beyond normal casting-distance creates several problems. However, these obstacles can, with a little patience, be overcome, although often at the expense of accuracy. At long range this is to be expected and does not really matter. Provided that the bait is dropped into deep water, it is immaterial whether it is directly in front of the swim or not. A boat, of course, is one answer, but few angling clubs or riparian owners allow the use of a boat because of the obvious danger involved should an accident occur well away from the bank.

One of the simplest methods of increasing effective casting-range is to buy a wide-spooled, sea-sized, fixed-spool reel. I say wide-spooled as many of these reels are fitted with deep, narrow spools which hold plenty of line but empty rapidly during casting, and this drastically cuts down casting distance. With a wide spool this problem does not occur and distance-casting can be achieved. Originally these big reels were designed to hold heavy line for beach fishing, but by backing up the spool with old line and then adding 200 yards (180 m) of 12 lb (5.4 kg) bs line to fill the spool correctly, these reels are perfectly adaptable for use in fresh water. Another advantage with these large reels is that the increased overall size of the reel makes for a rapid retrieving rate, and it is thus extremely simple to keep in direct contact with a fast-moving fish hooked in deep water.

Deadbait is the only natural bait suitable for this long-range deep-water work and where casting-power alone is to get the bait out, a substantial rod is essential. Short rods are useless for this sort of fishing and you will need a rod with a minimum length of 10 ft (3 m). Most pike specialists make up their own rods from hollow glass beach-caster blanks, which are normally obtainable in lengths of 11 to 12 ft (3.3–3.6 m). Extra-large rod rings are needed for use with a sea-sized, fixed-spool reel. Small-diameter rings are useless and will only cut down the casting potential of the rod. When using the long-range tactics, great care must be taken when striking, for with a line of 12 lb (5.4 kg) breaking strain it is very easy to break up on the strike. To some extent the elasticity of the line will cushion the strike, but even so it is advisable to be as gentle as possible.

Legered livebaits

Livebaiting with float tackle is not always the most practical method of fishing. There are occasions when it is advisable to dispense entirely with the float and use a plain running leger to present the bait to the fish. Of course, legering can be an extremely boring way of fishing and many anglers prefer to float-fish simply because it is far more pleasant to sit and contemplate a brightly coloured float than it is to sit gazing at a line stretching between rod tip and water. There are occasions, however, when the use of a float will ruin any chance of sport. This applies particularly to heavily-fished waters, where most of the pike have at one time or another been caught and have learned to drop a bait if it is suspended beneath a large buoyant float. A bait presented on leger tackle will not frighten the fish and because of this a leger is by far the most practical method to employ. The leger is also useful for fishing river swims where a float would drag the bait into an obstruction or away from a likely pike lie. There is nothing complicated about a pike leger (see Fig. 43) which is made the same as a normal running leger.

(Fig. 43)

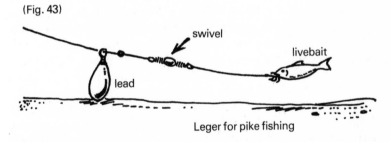

Leger for pike fishing

There are numerous methods of attaching a livebait. The two most practical are, to lip-hook the bait on one prong of a treble hook or to make up a special snap tackle and hook the bait through the lip and the back (see Fig. 44). This is the best method if long casting is necessary; but a livebait hooked in this way dies quickly, whereas a lip-hooked bait remains alive for hours on end. The distance between lead and bait should be approximately 2 ft (60 cm) but longer and shorter traces can be used without adverse effect on the sport. With a double-hook

(Fig. 44)

A two-hook snap tackle must be used
to hook livebait if long casting is necessary

rig, an early strike can be made with confidence. Where one treble hook is used, it is essential to give a pike time to take the bait well into its mouth before you strike and set the hook.

When to strike at a taking pike

When a pike picks up a bait it will move off on its first run, the length of this varying from about 3 ft–90 ft (0.9–27 m) or more. After this initial surge the fish will stop and turn the bait so that it can be swallowed head first. Once the fish begins to move away for the second time it is safe to assume that the bait is well inside its mouth and the strike should be made accordingly. Any further delay will result in the fish being hooked deep inside its throat, and this will probably mean that it will have to be destroyed before the hook or hooks can be retrieved.

How to strike at a pike

In most forms of angling a firm upward strike is essential. In pike fishing, striking in this fashion is a mistake, as a pike's mouth is both bony and tooth-filled and an upward strike will cause the hooks to bounce off these bones and teeth. The only safe hook-hold is the corner of the mouth which, being gristly, offers firm purchase for a hook. It is necessary, therefore, to strike sideways and in the opposite direction to that in which the fish is moving. If the pike runs off to the right, then the strike should be made to the left: if the fish makes off to the left, then swing the rod round to the right and drive the hook solidly home from that direction. A pike cleanly hooked in the corner of its jaw will seldom escape by biting through the trace as the wire will be clear of its teeth.

Methods of landing pike

There was a time when all caught pike were automatically destroyed, regardless of size or weight. During this period a gaff was always used to land the fish. Nowadays these instruments are rarely used. A gaff can be a lethal instrument, and because of this many forward-looking angling societies stipulate that gaffs must not be employed under any circumstances. This, in many ways, is a wise ruling for even an expert can make a mis-timed strike with a gaff and drive the gaff-hook into the body of a good fish. Once this has happened, the pike has little chance of recovering from its wound.

Most pike fishermen prefer to dispense entirely with the gaff and use a carp-sized landing net for the larger fish. This is a far more humane method and is to be strongly recommended.

Extracting the hooks

Pike have large teeth and strong jaws which can inflict a nasty wound. Because of this, a medium-sized pike gag (see Fig. 45)

(Fig. 45)

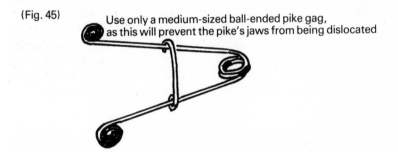

Use only a medium-sized ball-ended pike gag, as this will prevent the pike's jaws from being dislocated

should always be carried. The very large pike gags should have no place in the pike angler's bag, for they are brutal and over-powerful instruments which easily dislocate the jaws of even the biggest pike. Special pike gags with rounded ends are now available and should be used. Failing this, the points on a standard pike gag can be filed down or, better still, dipped in Araldite, to prevent them from digging into the mouth of the fish. Once the gag is in position, the catch can be slipped and the jaws of the fish prised open. A long disgorger or surgical forceps (see Fig. 46) can then be used to extract the hook or hooks. In the case of a lightly-hooked fish this operation is simple, but if the hooks are lodged in the back of the pike's throat the angler is faced with either trying to probe for the hooks or else cutting the trace as close to the hooks as possible and releas-ing the pike complete with hooks, in the hope that it will

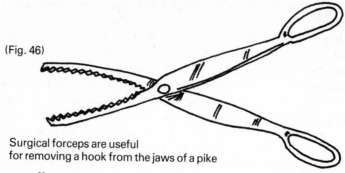

(Fig. 46)

Surgical forceps are useful
for removing a hook from the jaws of a pike

eventually manage to get rid of them and recover. This last method is extremely unsatisfactory, which is why so many anglers prefer to use the easily-removable barbless hooks.

Deadbaiting

As mentioned, pike are lazy fish and the larger they grow the less inclined they become to hunt actively. Instead, they become scavengers living for the most part on dead fish from the bottom. On hard-fished waters, pike are well supplied with food of this kind, for the mortality rate of fish that have been handled and confined to keepnets is high. Pike become used to finding an ample supply of easily-obtainable food and lose their hunting instincts and thus show more interest in deadbaits than in live ones.

Deadbait fishing is a highly selective method, for as a rule very large baits are used and because of this and the fact that big pike are basically scavengers, the average size of a pike which falls to deadbait is far higher than the average weight of a fish taken by livebaiting or spinning. As a pike is capable of swallowing a fish practically as large as itself there are exceptions, but as a rule only pike close to or over 10 lb (4.5 kg) in weight take deadbaits. Deadbaiting is a comparatively slow method of fishing and any angler wishing to concentrate on this technique must be prepared to spend many inactive and fishless hours.

Providing it is large and reasonably fresh, almost any fish will make a good deadbait, irrespective of whether it is a fresh-water or sea-water species. On hard-fished waters where the pike have become cautious of whole fish-bait, half or even quartered bait will often produce plenty of fish. Some anglers use whole sprats as bait. It is my experience that these make excellent bait for small pike but seldom attract the big fish.

Big pike being true cannibals are quite prepared to eat their own offspring. A 39 lb (17.7 kg) pike was caught on a deadbait pike estimated to weigh 4–5 lb (1.8–2.3 kg), an example of the cannibalistic tendencies of big pike. A week or two before this huge fish was landed, a Norfolk angler successfully boated a 40 lb (18.1 kg) pike which had accepted a dead roach. These fish, which were two of the largest pike ever caught in this country, both fell to deadbaits, proving that as a big-fish technique deadbait-fishing has a great deal to recommend it.

Deadbaiting with float tackle

Pike will take deadbaits on or off the bottom, and under certain circumstances a deadbait suspended 1–2 ft (0.3–0.6 m) off the bottom can be highly effective. On windy days when the water's surface is disturbed, a bait mounted on snap tackle (see Fig. 47) so that it hangs below the float as naturally as possible will often produce more bites than a deadbait fished on leger tackle. This is probably due to the motion of the water which causes the bait to work up and down.

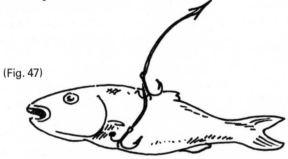

(Fig. 47)

A deadbait fixed to snap tackle, for use on a windy day

Laying-on with float tackle

This is a technique closely akin to the conventional leger tackle normally employed by deadbait users. The float serves no useful purpose other than as a bite indicator and because of this small floats are best used. In waters where the pike have learned to pick the bait up cautiously, a float is the ideal bite detector to use. Provided that the float is set to sit at half-cock on the water (see Fig. 48), the slightest pull on the bait will be clearly registered. On standard leger tackle this initial pull could well go completely unnoticed. The float leger is best used in water no more than 10-15 ft (3-4.6 m) in depth. Over this depth the tackle can become rather unmanageable. In swims that are thickly carpeted with weed, the float not only acts as a bite indicator but also keeps the line between terminal tackle and rod tip above the weed (see Fig. 49). With a standard leger the

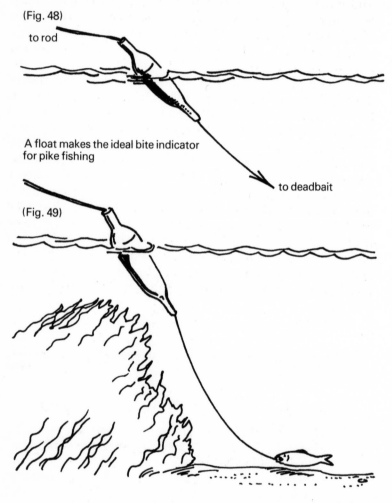

(Fig. 48)

to rod

A float makes the ideal bite indicator for pike fishing

to deadbait

(Fig. 49)

It can also be used to keep the line above the weed level

line would quickly sink into the weed, which would make striking on bite detection almost impossible. The line should be rubbed over with a wax floatant for all forms of float fishing.

Legered deadbait

This is the simplest and the best all-round method of deadbait fishing, a technique which is widely used by pike specialists all over Europe. Obviously a bait presented on leger tackle is intended to lie right on the bottom. Consequently no float should be used, nor for that matter is a lead necessary, for the weight of the deadbait is quite sufficient for casting purposes. Freshly-caught deadbaits will float unless their swim bladders are broken. This can be achieved by running a baiting-needle through the bladder area. Probably the most important part of the deadbait tackle is the trace. This is normally made up as follows: take 2 ft (60 cm) of braided or nylon-covered wire of 12–15 lb (5.4–6.8 kg) breaking strain. Tie a single-barrel swivel to one end and then slide a size 1 or 1–0 single-eyed hook and a size 4 or 6 treble hook on to the wire. Now tie a treble of corresponding size to the loose end of the wire, and the trace is complete (see Fig. 50). The bait should be mounted so that it hangs head down with one treble on either side of its body. To do this, the trace should be wound round the bait. The single hook should be inserted into the root of the bait's tail and, if necessary, secured with two or three twists of copper wire. The bait is then ready for use (see Fig. 51). The single hook serves no useful purpose except to hold the bait securely during casting.

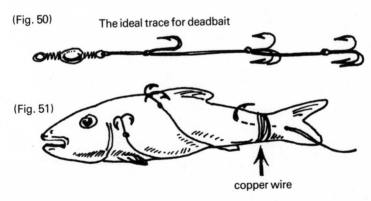

(Fig. 50)   The ideal trace for deadbait

(Fig. 51)

copper wire

Deadbait mounted on a trace and secured with copper wire

Deadbaits are often rather soft and, unless firmly attached to the hooks, may easily tear free in mid-air.

Balanced deadbait

Large deadbaits are comparatively heavy and in waters which have a thick growth of blanket weed the bait may have a tendency to sink into this weed. To overcome this, two buoyant strips of cork or, better still, polystyrene should be lashed firmly to either side of the deadbait's tail (see Fig. 52). Trial and error will show just how much buoyancy should be added to a bait to make it balance correctly. A deadbait which is correctly balanced will sink slowly, head first and will come to rest on the weed, nose down. This makes it appear to be a naturally feeding fish. To make the bait even more natural, it should be mounted on the trace so that it hangs tail up, instead of head up as with normal deadbait tackle. The single hook should be passed through both lips of the bait, with the two treble hooks spaced accordingly. This will leave the tail section of the bait looking as natural as possible and the remainder of the trace and the reel line will lead away from the deadbait's head and thus be concealed by the weed fronds.

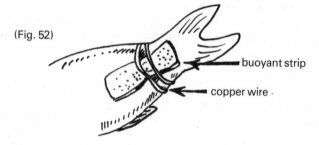

(Fig. 52)

buoyant strip

copper wire

Deadbait can be given buoyancy by lashing cork or polystyrene to its tail

Spinning

Pike respond well to artificial lures and a day's spinning can be a pleasant and rewarding pastime. The average size of pike caught on artificial baits is low, but there have been plenty of big pike caught on man-made lures. Last season I caught a beautiful 18 lb (8.2 kg) pike on an artificial lure. Some years before this I took a 19 lb (8.6 kg) pike on a home-made plug bait. Pits that hold extensive stocks of pike make the best venues for the spinning fisherman, for where pike are prolific and have to compete with each other for food, sport can usually be relied upon; although even the most productive pike fisheries have their 'off' days when nothing seems to interest the fish. One of the best things about spinning is that it keeps you on the move and allows you to cover a vast amount of water during the course of a day. Spinning also allows one to travel light, with just a small shoulder bag to hold spare lures, food and a landing net clipped to the shoulder-bag strap.

Artificial lures are legion and many anglers tend to collect them almost as a hobby. This is a mistake, for carrying a vast selection of assorted artificial baits there is a temptation to change to a new bait every few casts, in a vain attempt to find a lure that will attract the pike. This is wrong, far too much time will be spent switching baits instead of fishing, and for this reason it is advisable to carry a small selection of carefully chosen practical lures. The best lures are usually made in Sweden or America. Silver-coloured lures work best in clear water, and copper-coloured baits are most effective in dirty dark water. Because of this, it pays to carry two or three baits of each colour, or buy the baits that are finished with silver on one side and copper on the other.

Deep and slow is an adage often applied to pike spinning and a very true one it is, for pike often refuse a bait that spins rapidly along at the mid-water mark but take it with confidence if it flashes slowly along close to the bottom. Extra movement can be imparted to the bait by raising or lowering the rod tip at irregular intervals or by moving the rod tip from side to side. By slowing up the rate of retrieve or stopping it momentarily, the bait will pause or flutter down like a sick or wounded fish. This movement definitely adds to the attractiveness of the bait. Pike sometimes hook themselves when they take a spinner, but it is advisable to strike at any check to the forward motion of the bait.

Spinning with a natural bait

This is a popular method among Norfolk pike fishermen, but one that is seldom used by gravel-pit anglers, despite the fact that a carefully-spun natural bait can be a deadly lure for pike of all sizes. Roach, dace, gudgeon, sprats and small herrings all make good natural spinning baits, although freshly-killed fish are probably best as their flesh is still firm, whereas the flesh of sea fish may well be soft, which means that it will tear off the hooks or break up completely in a very short time.

Natural baits should be mounted on a specially constructed spinning flight or on wobbling tackle (see Fig. 53). These, if used correctly, will impart just the right degree of spin or wobble to a dead fish. A wobbled natural bait is probably the better of the two methods, but both are highly effective. A wobbled bait must be worked very slowly across the pit bed and should be allowed to settle to the bottom at regular intervals. This will often cause a following pike to pick up the bait, presumably it thinks that, in some way, it has managed to kill the fish during the chase. This technique is similar in many respects to the straightforward deadbaiting methods described earlier. A pike will hang on for longer to a spun natural bait than it will to an artificial lure, which gives more time to set the hooks.

(Fig. 53)

Wobbling tackle, for use when spinning deadbait

Roach

Good roach fishing is not easy to come by. Roach like many types of coarse fish, have peak periods which last for a few seasons before stocks rapidly decline. During the past decade roach have been on the decline. The signs are, however, that roach stocks are now increasing and prospects look good for the future. Roach like ultra-clear water and seem to grow best in large reservoirs or gravel pits. Ideally, from the specimen hunting point of view, these waters should contain minimal stocks of roach which can then grow at maximum speed. Waters that are full of 4-6 oz (0.1-0.17 kg) roach are unlikely to yield any fish of specimen size, for roach like perch are prolific breeders and quickly become stunted as a result of over-breeding. Waters that hold big roach seldom give up their secrets easily, although when a roach is caught from one of these waters it will usually be a big one. Some years ago I fished a gravel pit of this type that was reputed to hold roach of over 3 lb (1.4 kg) in weight, although none had been caught for some years. I spent six months chasing these elusive fish for very mediocre results and then, during a heavy snow storm, a roach of 2 lb 8 oz (1.13 kg) took my legered bait. Later in the year I went on to take other roach of specimen size from the same pit but never in quantity; my best day's catch being made up of 14 fish weighing between 1 lb 8 oz and 2 lb 6½ oz (0.68 and 1.1 kg). Many expert roach anglers have spent a lifetime trying to catch a roach of over 2 lb (0.9 kg) in weight.

Any roach weighing 1 lb (0.45 kg) or over can be regarded as a good fish, and anything over 1½ lb (0.7 kg) as a specimen, a 2-pounder (0.9 kg) being a very big roach indeed. Big roach should always be carefully examined, particularly if they are approaching record size, as roach often cross with rudd and bream and although a big fish may have the appearance of a true roach there is always the possibility that it is, in fact, a hybrid and not a true roach at all. There have been a number of record or near-record roach recorded during the past few years, which when carefully examined by an expert have proved to be hybrid fish. Usually, a careful examination of the fish will show slight differences. For example, roach/rudd hybrids are often deeper and a little more golden than true roach, while the anal-fin shape usually shows the difference between roach and roach/bream crosses, for the fin of the hybrid is more elongated than that of a true roach. If in doubt get a second and, where possible, qualified opinion. This may mean killing the fish, a job no true angler will relish but a job which is essential if a near-record fish is to be positively identified.

A big fish is, of course, usually nearing the end of its life and this may be a comfort to any angler faced with making the decision to kill a very big and very beautiful fish. Where possible, two scales should be taken from the shoulder of any big roach and these scales submitted to a scale-reading expert.

From these scales an experienced ichthyologist can determine the age and the growth rate of the fish. Information of this kind can be invaluable to both the angler who caught the fish and the owners of the water from which it came. A 2 lb 8 oz (1.13 kg) roach I caught from a sand pit was estimated to be ten years old, proving that the fish had grown fairly rapidly and, more important still, that the fish in the pit in question were capable of reaching a weight of at least 3 lb (1.4 kg), for roach can continue to grow until they reach an age of approximately fifteen years.

As luck would have it, I have never managed to get a bigger roach from the water although, on several occasions, I have been fortunate enough to watch huge roach swim quietly through my swim. These fish would, I am sure, have topped the 3 lb (1.4 kg) mark, though it is extremely difficult accurately to judge the weight of fish seen in water. I can, however, remember clearly how big my best roach looked as it came into the net and the free-swimming roach I saw were larger than my own fish when viewed from a similar position and distance. Big roach, of course, are noted for their inbred cunning and it is rare for the average angler to land a roach of anywhere near specimen proportions. Oddly enough, big roach can often be found in waters that contain a large head of pike. Although the pike eat vast amounts of roach, the fish that are left have an ample supply of food and grow to a large size. I know of one lake in Hampshire which contains hundreds of pike, some of them topping the 30 lb (13.6 kg) mark. Catches of a dozen or more good pike are common at this pit and yet it also yields large bags of specimen roach to the patient and competent angler. This will probably surprise many of the anti-pike brigade, who are convinced that pike and other coarse fish simply will not mix, but it only goes to show that fish which are preyed upon by large predators often reach a good weight simply because they are continually being weeded out. This is really nature's way of selective growth and as the weak fish and many of the fry are destroyed in huge numbers the prime fish are given sufficient room to develop to the full.

Feeding habits

Roach are basically a bottom-feeding species but there are occasions when roach will rise, sometimes right up to the surface, in search of food. This reversal of normal feeding pattern only occurs during hot weather when the oxygen content of the water is low or when the surface of the water is thick with spent insect life, upon which the roach can feed; the smaller roach are more prone to this surface feeding than big fish. Roach live for the most part on various types of insects: caddis grub, nymphs and larvae being the mainstay of their diet. Roach will also eat worms, weed, bread and cereal whenever these are available. They will also eat small water snails and tiny swan mussels. Very big roach occasionally show a predatory streak, and more than one 2 lb (0.9 kg) roach has been taken on a live minnow intended for perch. Many fish show these cannibalistic tendencies, usually just after the spawning period when the water is thick with small fry.

Baits

Maggot is the most widely-used of all coarse-fishing baits and one of the most popular of all roach baits. The roach is predominantly an insect eater and shows a marked preference for caddis grubs, which maggots closely resemble. Loose maggots can also be used to 'groundbait' a swim. Although roach of all sizes will accept a hook baited with a large bunch of maggots, the bigger fish are more likely to accept a single or double maggot bait, as these look more natural than the bunched baits. Match anglers have bred a wide variety of maggots, many of which are dyed exotic colours, pink, red, lime, green and yellow being the most popular shades. Many matchmen are convinced that these unnaturally-coloured grubs are better fish catchers than the plain undyed maggot, and this may be true when the bait is being used on heavily-fished waters, where fish have learned to associate the natural maggot with danger.

To make the maggot bait appear as natural as possible to the fish the hook point should be passed just under the skin of the blunt end of the maggot (see Fig. 54). Under no circumstances should the maggot be threaded on to the hook. This not only destroys their natural appearance it also kills them.

(Fig. 54)

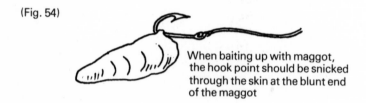

When baiting up with maggot, the hook point should be snicked through the skin at the blunt end of the maggot

Few anglers realise that a lively redworm or brandling is one of the finest of all roach baits, consequently it is rare to see worms being used by roach fishermen. My own largest roach was taken on a lively redworm and I have every confidence in worms where roach are concerned. The smaller worms appear to be most effective for still-water roach fishing, possibly because pits often contain vast numbers of bloodworms which the small redworms closely resemble. I have, however, taken roach to 1 lb 14 oz (0.85 kg) on the tail end of a lobworm. When worm is used as bait, it is advisable to refrain from groundbaiting with whole worms, although a few chopped worms mixed in with mashed bread or bran groundbait helps to attract fish.

Roach are very fond of bread-based baits and will feed readily on crust, flake or paste. As crust and flake are soft baits, which can be quickly torn from the hooks, it is essential to strike at the slightest indication of a bite when using either of these baits, otherwise the fish will immediately suck the bait from the hook.

Paste is a more substantial bait and can be most effective. The best paste is made from the crumbs of a day-old loaf. This should be mixed with water and carefully kneaded to the right consistency in a clean cloth. Heavy smokers will be well advised to wash their hands thoroughly in pit water before baiting up. Observing points like this can make all the difference to a day's fishing. Paste can be flavoured with honey or coloured by including custard powder.

Hempseed is without doubt the most killing of all known roach baits. Hemp was originally introduced into this country just before or just after the start of World War 1, and has proved so deadly that many angling societies ban its use on their waters. Uncooked hempseed can be purchased from tackle dealers and pet shops. Before it can be used the raw hemp must be boiled in a saucepan full of water until the individual grains split showing the white kernel of the seed. Once this has occurred the water should be strained off and the hemp left to cool. The cooling process can be hastened by washing the seed under cold water. Once cool, the hemp should be placed in a bait tin or, better still, a linen bag. Never prepare hempseed more than twenty-four hours in advance, for the seed has a tendency to go sour if left unused for two or three days. By adding a dash of soda to the boiling water the hemp can be darkened, which may make it more attractive to the fish. When baiting up with hemp, the hookbend should be pushed gently into the crack in the seed (see Fig. 55); never thread the seed on to the hook, for this will mar the penetration of the hook point when the strike is made.

(Fig. 55)

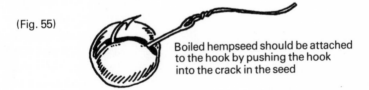

Boiled hempseed should be attached to the hook by pushing the hook into the crack in the seed

Other baits

Cheese cubes are a first-class but little-used bait. These are often effective on waters where roach treat the more conventional baits with caution. Cheddar or processed cheese is best. Cheese can also be mixed into bread paste. Roach presumably come to this bait because of its smell. Big roach are also partial to tinned sweetcorn; a bait which many species of fish find attractive.

Location

Unlike bream, roach seldom give away their whereabouts by rolling or priming on the surface, consequently a period of trial and error is often required to locate a swim which the roach shoals visit regularly. Deepish gravelly-bottomed swims, particularly those with shallow water on either side (see Fig. 56) often produce good catches. Deep holes close to sheltered areas of bank often fish well, especially in the late evening when roach shoals move out of the rapidly cooling shallows and begin to drop back into the deeper and warmer water. Beds of surface weed do not seem to attract roach, although beds of sunken lilies, or 'cabbage patches' as they are usually called, are often ideal places to find and catch big roach. Roach seldom venture far from deep water in winter and unless there has been a prolonged period of mild weather, the winter-roach angler will be well advised to concentrate on the deeper swims.

(Fig. 56)

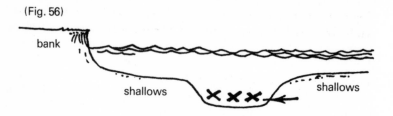

Roach will often collect in gravelly-bottomed holes

Tackle
Rods

There are dozens of rods available to the roach angler, most of which are quite suitable for general roach fishing.

For general float fishing a long rod is advisable. This can be made of hollow fibreglass or carbon fibre and should have an easy action. This means that the rod should be supple enough to cast a light float a fair distance and pliable enough to pick up a long line when the strike has to be made. The ideal roach rod is between 12 and 14 ft (3.6 and 4.3 m) in length, although for the shorter angler, an 11-12 ft (3.3-3.6 m) rod may be more comfortable. The same rod can also be used for light leger work.

Reels

Although a centre-pin reel is quite useful for fishing the bankside swims, a fixed-spool reel is more versatile and is unsurpassed for general fishing.

Lines

Fine lines are essential for roach fishing. For float fishing a line with a 2-3 lb (0.9-1.4 kg) breaking strain is the heaviest that should be employed. It is noticeable that when a heavier line is used there is a sharp decline in the number of bites received per session. This is understandable for roach are line-shy fish and will eject a suspect bait at the slightest indication that all is not as it should be.

Hooks

Roach have small mouths and show a preference for small baits so it is advisable to choose one's hooks carefully. For hempseed, single maggot or other very small baits a size 16 hook is best; while for bread, wheat or bunched maggot baits sizes 12 to 14 are most suitable; for worms a size 8 or 10 hook should be used, depending upon the size of the worm. Round-bend hooks with fine points are best for roach fishing. Whether or not one buys loose-eyed or spade-end hooks or hooks tied to a length of nylon is a matter of personal choice. For most fish I prefer to buy loose hooks and tie them directly to the reel line, but for roach I prefer to use the tied-to-nylon variety, mainly because hooks of this kind are neatly tied and very sharp.

Floats

Peacock quills make beautiful roach floats. These are obtainable from any tackle shop but are, unfortunately, usually highly varnished. This flashiness may be attractive to the human eye, but can be very off-putting for the fish. For this reason, it is advisable to paint over the lower section of the float with a matt green or brown paint. An antenna float is the best type to use in rough water, for these floats are designed to ride steadily in even the most disturbed water. For fast-water work trotting floats should be used (see **Fig. 57**). Whenever possible a roach float should be attached by the bottom end only, as this makes the float more sensitive.

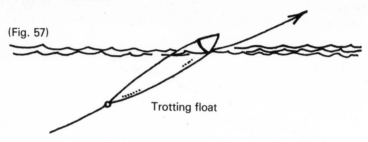

(Fig. 57)

Trotting float

Weights

When float fishing, split shot, mouse dropping and olivette weights should be used to cock the float. For leger work, small arlsey bombs make the best pattern weights.

Methods

Float fishing

Roach live and feed close to the bottom, this means that light float tackle, set so that the bait just trips or lays on the bottom (see **Fig. 58**) can be used to good effect while roach fishing. Only the lightest of floats should be used, for roach will seldom take a bait suspended beneath a heavy float. Quills are ideal, but cork or balsa-bodied floats can be used provided that the size of the body is kept within reasonable bounds. For fishing deep still waters that are open to the wind, a double-bodied float (see

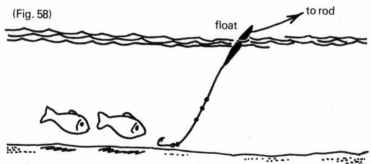

(Fig. 58)

to rod

float

Present your bait close to the bottom when fishing for roach

Fig. 59) can be most useful. The stability of this type of float is extremely good and even in the strongest of winds these floats can be relied upon to remain steady. This is very important as a bait which continually bobs up and down will catch few fish.

(Fig. 59)

Double-bodied float

Fishing with hempseed

Roach of all sizes love to feed on hempseed and on many waters where hemp is used consistently the resident roach become so addicted to this seed that they will often completely ignore all other baits. Because of this some angling clubs stipulate in their rule books that no angler shall use this deadly bait. On roach waters where the use of hempseed is permissible a day's 'hemping' can be most productive, although far from relaxing as bites on hempseed are normally very fast affairs and complete concentration and co-ordination are required to connect with them; even an expert hemp fisherman is lucky to hook one in three bites and the average angler trying hemp for the first time will miss at least $\frac{3}{4}$ of the bites indicated by the float. The reflex striking action takes time to develop, but constant practice will soon perfect the striking technique. In waters where hemp is regularly used, very little groundbait will be required to attract the roach shoals, but on waters where hemp is a comparatively new bait it may be necessary to feed the swim regularly with loose seed. Once the fish begin to feed, the quantity of groundbait should gradually be decreased so that the fish have to hunt for their food. It is advisable, however, to throw out a few grains of hemp every time a fish is hooked. This will stop the shoal from breaking up.

Once the fish are right on feed, they will take anything that vaguely resembles a grain of hemp. Split shot come into this category and many false bites will be registered if shot are used to cock the float. To overcome this, a small coil of lead wire stopped at either end by a dust shot should be used as a weight (see Fig. 60), the shot being placed right against the wire, so that the whole weight becomes a neat package. For extra sensitivity the float should be attached by the bottom end only, and weighted so that only a tiny section projects above the surface (see Fig. 57). This is most important as bites for hemp are very sharp and, unless the float is well shotted, many of the bites will barely make the float dip. If the tackle is set properly, however, each bite will pull the float completely under the water, making bite detection much simpler. Tiny quill floats are the best for hemping, a 3 in (7.5 cm) length of peacock quill being easily as sensitive as the more elaborate floats on the market, and costing a fraction of the price.

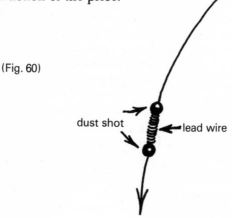

(Fig. 60)

dust shot

lead wire

Lead wire should be used for weight when fishing for roach, this prevents roach mistaking widely-spaced dust shot for hempseed

It may be necessary to alter the distance between float and hook on a number of occasions while hemp fishing as shoaling roach have a tendency to change their feeding-levels fairly frequently. A cessation of regular bites indicates that the fish have done this and that the tackle needs adjustment. It occasionally pays to fish right on the bottom as the very big roach will sometimes accept hemp bait fished in this way while ignoring it if fished in the conventional manner. Although no-one really knows why roach take hemp so well, there is a theory that hempseed bears a resemblance to a small watersnail upon which the roach feed. Other cereal baits can be used but seem to lack the deadliness of the hemp.

Like many fish, roach are semi-nocturnal and will feed well throughout the night. Oddly enough, few anglers deliberately fish for roach at night, although those who do are often rewarded with first-class catches. My experience of night fishing for big roach has been rather limited but I have caught some big roach after dark, including fish of 2 lb 2½ oz and 2 lb 1 oz (0.97 and 0.93 kg).

During the warmer months roach shoals often venture into shallow water during the night. Because of this it is advisable to concentrate on swims of medium-depth. A plain running leger should be used for roach fishing at night. Flake from the inside of a new loaf seems to make the best bait, but crust can also be used to good effect. Few anglers ever consider night fishing after the end of September even though big roach often feed well during the early part of a winter night. The air temperatures often rise slightly as darkness falls and this rise of temperature brings the roach shoals on feed.

During the colder months roach seldom wander far from the deep water. As they seem to dislike mud and silt, the ideal swim is one with a bottom composed of clean gravel.

Winter days are short and by staying on at the waterside until eight or nine o'clock at night some extraordinarily good fishing can be had without too much personal discomfort. After about nine o'clock, however, the temperature starts to drop rapidly and the fish normally cease feeding.

Rudd

The rudd is a mainly still-water fish which thrives extremely well in lakes, broads and gravel pits. A big rudd is a beautiful golden-bronze with bright crimson fins which set off the coppery sheen of its flanks to perfection.

There is another variety of rudd which is sometimes caught from waters that hold the more normal specimens. These fish, although golden in colour, have lemon-coloured fins instead of crimson ones. Amateur anglers often confuse rudd with roach; this is understandable as both fish are rather similar in basic appearance. The simplest method of identification is to look at the mouth of the fish. If the lower lip recedes it is a roach; if the lip protrudes it is a rudd. Also, the lips of the true rudd are darker in colour than those of a roach. There are, of course, hybrids between the two species. Rudd grow to a slightly larger size than roach, and the rod-caught record is $4\frac{1}{2}$ lb (2.04 kg). Any rudd over 2 lb (0.9 kg) in weight can be regarded as a specimen, and those of over 3 lb (1.4 kg) in weight as outstanding fish. Big rudd are few and far between, although I once caught eighteen rudd of over 2 lb (0.9 kg) in weight at one sitting; an achievement I never expect to repeat, as rudd of this size are rarely encountered in such quantity. Despite their deep, powerful build, rudd are rather delicate fish and are quick to die if confined for any great length of time in a keepnet.

Feeding habits

The rudd is essentially a surface-feeding fish which obtains much of its food from the underside of floating weed pads or from submerged reed stalks. On warm evenings, when the rudd are feeding off the surface, the loud sucking noise they make with their mouths can be used to locate the shoals. Big rudd occasionally feed right on the bottom, like roach. This usually occurs in shallow water, or during the winter months.

Baits

All the usual roach baits can be used to take rudd, but for the bigger fish large worms or big pieces of bread make the best bait. Walnut-sized pieces of bread flake are by no means too big for large rudd to take, for these fish are able to open their mouths far wider than roach of similar size. Maggots can also be used as bait but, being small, they attract the attention of the smaller fish which are more active and less discerning than the bigger rudd.

In Europe, particularly in Holland, roach, rudd and bream anglers regard spinning as a standard technique. These continental anglers catch large numbers of big fish on spinning tackle, and have developed a special technique to take bream, roach, rudd and hybrids.

Ultra-light tackle is used for this type of fishing. Tiny fibreglass spinning rods, minute fixed-spool reels and lines with a 1 lb (0.45 kg) breaking strain are used as a matter of course. The artificial lures used are tiny baits, designed on the bar-spoon principle, with the treble hook hidden by a tuft of red wool. These baits are obviously intended to look like roach or rudd fry, which backs up the theory that both these fish have cannibalistic tendencies. The method of fishing with these lures is interesting. The baits seem to work best when fished over a clear bottom, close to, or in between, thick beds of weed. Having selected a suitable swim, the angler casts out, waits for the bait to touch the bottom and then begins to retrieve the bait fairly rapidly. After a yard or two of line has been wound back on to the reel spool, the bait is allowed to flutter down to the bottom, where it is left for anything up to five minutes before the whole process is repeated. Bites tend to occur when the bait is stationary, proving that not only are the roach, rudd and bream predatory, they are also scavengers, willing to pick up and eat any small dead fish that come their way. To my knowledge no-one in this country has tried using artificial baits for rudd fishing.

Being surface breeders rudd do not respond well to groundbait. Even lightly-mixed groundbait, which breaks up as soon as it hits the surface and forms a cloud of slowly sinking bait particles, will seldom hold the attention of rudd for any appreciable length of time. There is only one suitable groundbaiting technique, the anchored crust method (see Fig. 61), which can be used in any swim, irrespective of wind or other climatic conditions. There is nothing new about this technique, for it has been used for years by rudd experts on the Norfolk Broads. It is, however, a most useful method of concentrating the rudd shoal into a relatively small area. The bait is a thick piece of stale or toasted breadcrust, tied to a length of string to which a stone or iron bolt has been attached. This weight serves to anchor the

(Fig. 61)

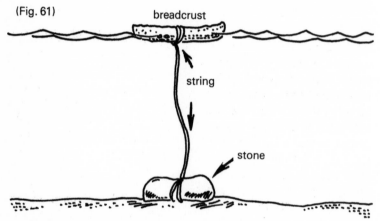

The anchored breadcrust method of groundbaiting is very successful for rudd

crust in the swim. To allow for drift, it is essential to determine accurately the depth of the swim and then allow an extra 18 in (0.45 m) of string between anchor weight and crust. If the string between weight and crust is too taut, the buoyancy of the bread will lift the weight and cause the whole lot to drift out of the swim. Under no circumstances should nylon be used as an anchor line, for nylon is practically invisible both in and out of the water, and a loose length of nylon may kill or maim a water bird. Worse still, nylon does not rot and consequently it can kill over and over again. Once the rudd begin to nuzzle at the crust, then light float tackle, baited with bread, worm or maggot can be cast directly at the crust so that the bait falls naturally among the hungry fish.

Dry groundbait

Small quantities of dry groundbait poured directly on to wind-ruffled water will quickly spread and form a wide patch of floating bait particles. By pouring 6–7 lb (2.7–3.2 kg) of groundbait into the water, a very large surface area can be covered with a film of bait, which will attract and hold the attention of the rudd shoals without actually feeding them. By using light float-tackle set so that the bait is suspended just beneath the surface it is possible to catch large numbers of rudd as they swim beneath the film of floating groundbait.

Location

Rudd shoals seldom venture far from cover and the best rudd swims are usually situated close to beds of lily or other thick weed. Bankside swims beneath overhanging trees are also likely to hold rudd as a great deal of insect life will drop from the over-hanging foliage into the water below and rudd, like most fish, are quick to take advantage of a free supply of food. Even the tiniest patch of surface weed will attract rudd, particularly in the late evenings when the fish begin to rise steadily for the insects that hatch from beneath the leaves of the water weed. In open waters, where there are no weed beds or tree-shaded swims, the rudd shoals can often be located on the sunken sand bars and banks which usually divide the deep and the shallow water.

Tackle

Standard roach tackle can be used for most aspects of rudd fishing.

Methods

Float fishing

Rudd, being surface or semi-surface feeders, necessitate the use of float tackle to support the bait in the water. Rudd are shy fish and, where possible, only the lightest of tackle should be used. Self-cocking floats are best for rudd fishing (see Fig. 62) as rudd are quick to shy away from a line which has a string of split shot attached to it. A bait presented on self-cocking float tackle will sink at a natural speed which, in turn, will attract the attention of the rudd.

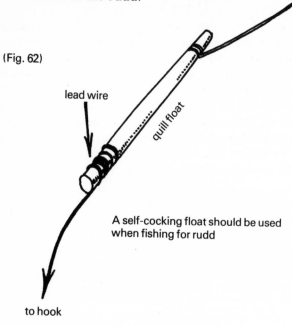

(Fig. 62)

lead wire

quill float

A self-cocking float should be used when fishing for rudd

to hook

Leger

Although rudd are usually fished with float tackle, they can be caught on a running leger; the leger being useful for fishing over areas of shallow water which are beyond the casting-range of float tackle.

Fly fishing

During periods of warm and settled weather, when the rudd shoals are actively engaged in hunting for spent insects on the surface of the water, the careful use of a dry-fly fishing outfit will produce plenty of action. Any light fly rod can be used for this game and the relatively cheap, but light, hollow-glass fly rods are ideal. The rod should be used in conjunction with a metal centre-pin reel and a plain, level fly line. More expensive tackle can be used, but as most coarse anglers will only use a fly rod on odd occasions it is best to keep the cost of such an outfit to an absolute minimum. Dark, hackled flies make the best lures but winged flies can be used as well. Rudd are bold risers, and take a fly in a manner that can be most exciting.

Winter rudd

Many anglers believe that rudd are exclusively a summer species and disappear during the colder months. This is, of course, nonsense, for rudd remain active throughout the winter, merely moving from their summer haunts to deeper waters where they often intermingle with the roach shoals. When the water temperature is low, the rudd shoals usually feed close to or actually on the bottom. Sport is at best spasmodic during the winter, but rudd will occasionally feed well at midday when the light is at its brightest. These fish will also feed after dark, and can be caught on similar tackle to roach.

Tench

The tench is a fish common to many areas. It varies considerably in colour from one water to another, but is normally either a beautiful golden bronze or a greeny-bronze colour. The eyes of a tench are red.

Two very beautiful variations of the tench also occur; one is the golden tench, the other is the extremely rare vermilion tench. Both are ornamental fish that have reverted to the wild state.

Tench are powerful sporting fish and are immensely popular with coarse anglers. Unfortunately, the productive tench-fishing season is comparatively short, the best sport being had during June and July. The fish also become active again in September and during October tench can be caught during periods of bright weather.

Feeding habits

Tench are almost exclusively bottom feeders and live mainly on the larvae of aquatic insects, on small swan mussels and on water snails. Very occasionally, tench will rise to the surface and suck down spent flies; at Tri-lake pits near Camberley in Surrey a number of tench have been taken on artificial flies intended for trout.

Baits

There are endless tench baits but for consistent success the tench angler will be well advised to fish with worm or bread baits, both of which make first-class tench lures. Large pieces of chopped swan-mussel flesh are another popular and quite successful tench bait. Swan mussels can be gathered by raking the bottom of the pit close to the bank with a fine-toothed rake. Maggots have accounted for a great many large tench and can be used to good effect in waters where there are no small fish. Bread can be used in several forms, both paste and flake being deadly big-tench baits. High protein baits (see Carp chapter) are becoming increasingly popular for tench fishing.

Location

Basically a still-water species, tench are most common in lakes and gravel pits, although some canals and a few slow rivers also hold good stocks of these fish.

Tench occasionally disclose their whereabouts by rolling on the surface but, more often than not, the angler will be forced to locate the fish by trying each likely-looking swim until tench are caught. Tench show a marked liking for heavy weed and swims adjacent to lily beds are well worth fishing. The shallowest swims are often the most productive during the early part of the season. Later, as the season advances, the fish have a tendency to work back into deeper water. Hungry tench are very active and spend a good deal of time rooting about on the bottom, where they send up clouds of frothy bubbles which show the observant angler just where to fish. Bubbling tench can usually be induced to take a bait; worm is particularly effective when tench are 'bubbling' in this fashion.

Tackle

Tench are strong and fight extremely well when hooked. Because of this it is advisable to use fairly powerful tackle when tench fishing.

Rods

Match and light bottom-fishing rods are useless for tench fishing. For all-round work you will need a carbon or hollow-glass 11 or 12 ft (3.3 or 3.6 m) Avon-type trotting rod. The easy progressive action of this kind of rod is used to the fullest extent while playing big tench. For legering, a slightly shorter rod can be used, the MKIV Avon-type rod being first-class for tench catching.

Reels

When float-fishing bankside swims, a good quality centre-pin reel is ideal for tench fishing. This kind of reel gives slightly more direct control over a hooked fish and, if used properly, can be a pleasure to fish with. Fixed-spool reels are more practical for legering or long-range work.

Lines

Many big tench have been taken on ultra-light lines by expert anglers, but most fishermen will be well advised to use a line with a breaking strain of at least 5 lb (2.3 kg). In thickly-weeded swims a line with a 7 lb (3.2 kg) breaking strain should be used, as there is little point in using a fine line if breakage is inevitable.

Hooks

A tench has a leathery mouth which affords good purchase for a hook, but strong hooks are essential as tench are heavy fish and can easily distort a hook constructed from thin-gauge wire. Sundridge specimen hooks, size 4, 6, 8 and 10 are the most useful hooks for tench fishing.

Floats

Tench are wary fish and they will drop a bait if they suspect that there is anything unnatural about it. Because of this, only the most delicate floats should be used. Quills are ideal, and light-bodied antenna floats are useful when fishing on windy days.

Methods

Float leger

Float legering (see Fig. 63) has always been a popular method with tench fishermen. The swan-shot float leger is an extremely sensitive set-up which, if properly adjusted, will clearly register the slightest bite.

The swan-shot float leger is a modified form of link leger. The distance between weights and hook should be kept to the minimum, and the float should be attached by the bottom end only and adjusted so that it just cocks nicely on the surface. Accurate plumbing of the depth of the water is essential if the tackle is to be set up perfectly. A small shot pinched on to the line directly beneath the float will help to balance the tackle correctly. To stop the line from dragging on the surface it is advisable to make certain that all the line between float and rod tip sinks. To do this, the cast should be made and then the rod tip should be sunk into the water and all the slack line wound in. Bites are clearly indicated by this kind of tackle which is well suited to use in large lakes or gravel pits.

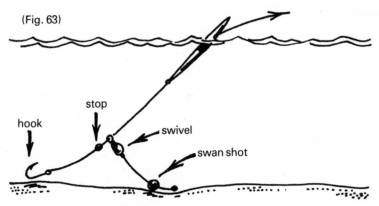

(Fig. 63)

hook

stop

swivel

swan shot

The swan-shot float leger

The lift method

This is one of the most popular methods of catching tench. Originally devised by the Taylor brothers of Aylesbury for use in local lakes, it is suitable for use in all still waters and requires no modification. The secret of the lift method (see Fig. 64) is to have the single swan shot situated no more than $1\frac{1}{2}$ in (3.8 cm) from the hook. Once again, it is essential to determine the depth of the swim extremely accurately and to set the float so that it sits upright in use, directly above the large shot which should rest on the bottom.

A biting fish will lift the shot off the bottom which, in turn, will cause the float to keel over (see figure). The lift method works in reverse to normal float-tackle method, for instead of the float being pulled under in the conventional fashion, it rises up and rests flat on the water's surface. The strike should be made when the float keels over. As with the swan-shot float leger, the lift float should be attached by the bottom end only. Quills make the best lift floats.

Free-line fishing

Tench respond well to baits presented on floatless leadless tackle, and for fishing bankside swims a worm or breadbait fished on this tackle can be most effective. Long casting is out of the question with this tackle as the weight of the bait is seldom heavy enough to cast any distance. Bites on the free line are usually indicated by the tightening or, alternatively, the falling slack, of the line between rod tip and water. A standard bite indicator can also be used.

Legering

Straightforward leger tackle is often the only practical method to use when attempting to fish swims situated beyond normal float or free-line casting range. When fishing over a muddy bottom a normal leger weight has a tendency to sink into the mud. To avoid this, a tube leger should be employed (see Fig. 65). The tube can be made from a standard plastic drinking-straw or a ball-point refill. The beauty of this type of leger is that even though the lead itself may become buried in mud, the tube holds the baited tackle above the mud and, most important of all, allows the line to run out freely when a fish takes the bait. The tube leger can also be used to combat heavy bottom weed.

Groundbaiting

Tench are a shoal fish which respond well to groundbait. Because of this, tench anglers who are able to visit their favourite waters regularly, make a point of pre-baiting their chosen swims prior to fishing. Bread, bran, mashed potato, sand and rice can all be used to make up groundbait. Ox blood mixed into the basic ingredients adds to the general attractiveness of the groundbait. Ox blood can be obtained from the local abattoir.

Tench are attracted to discoloured water, and before commencing to fish it is often advisable to rake the bottom of the pit thoroughly with a long-handled rake. This raking disturbs the silt and fills the water with all sorts of edible particles which attract the tench. Strangely enough, although a rake makes a considerable disturbance, the fish often move into the swim within an hour of it being raked. This is strange behaviour for a normally cautious species.

If the bottom is thick with water weed it pays to clear a hole with the rake so that the bait can rest on a clear bottom sur-

(Fig. 64)

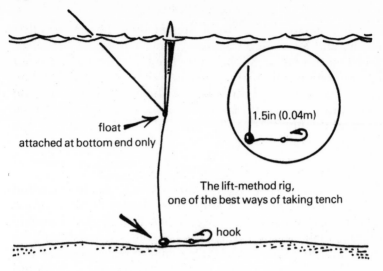

float
attached at bottom end only

1.5in (0.04m)

The lift-method rig,
one of the best ways of taking tench

hook

The float lifts and keels over as the fish picks up the bait
and so lifts the shot from the bottom

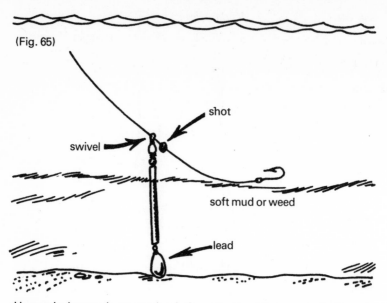

(Fig. 65)

shot

swivel

soft mud or weed

lead

Use a tube leger to keep your hook above the weed line or out of soft mud

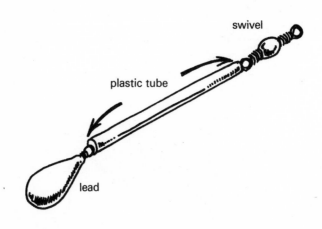

swivel

plastic tube

lead

rounded by thick weed. Tench find these cleared swims most
attractive and sport can be very good when a swim has been
dragged in this manner.

Night fishing

Dawn and dusk are normally the best times to catch tench, but night fishing can also be highly productive. Free-line fishing in bankside swims is the best method to employ, although it is possible to catch tench on float tackle at night provided that a torch is used to illuminate the swim.

Trout

During the past decade over a thousand still-water trout fisheries have been established in this country. These 'put and take' fisheries work on the day-ticket principle. The angler pays a set fee and is then allowed to catch four or six trout. Having reached this limit, the angler either purchases a second ticket or stops fishing.

Artificial though this may seem, this system enables the average angler to enjoy excellent fishing at a reasonable cost. Most of these fisheries are stocked with a mixture of brown and rainbow trout – some also contain American brook trout, or hybrid tiger trout which are a brown/brook trout cross. Other hybrids are found in one or two select waters but as yet these are not widespread in distribution. Fly fishing is the only method of angling allowed on all stocked waters. Many water authorities provide excellent fishing on reservoirs, Grafham, Rutland, Chew Magna and Blagdon are some of the finest examples of reservoir trout fishing.

In most counties in Great Britain there are rivers or streams that can be fished quite cheaply; there are even small overgrown brooks, holding vast heads of small sweet trout, that can be fished simply by asking permission at the adjacent farm house.

The size of brown trout depends entirely on the type of water and amount of food available to the fish. Moorland trout seldom exceed $\frac{1}{2}$ lb (0.23 kg) but in lowland rivers, where the trout have more food, 3 lb (1.4 kg) and above is considered to be a good specimen. The brown-trout record is held by an exceptional specimen weighing 17 lb 12 oz (8.05 kg) taken in Loch Faskally.

134

Feeding habits

Trout are mainly surface feeders and much of their food is taken in insect form, but on occasions they will become preoccupied with bottom feeding. At times like this they eat enormous quantities of small water snails and freshwater shrimps as well as worms and small fish.

Location

That fly fishing for trout is becoming increasingly popular, is due totally to the availability of day-ticket waters in all parts of the country. For those anglers not interested in the 'put and take' fisheries there are still many moorland streams, hill lochs and the like where wild brown trout can be caught on fly, worm or spinning tackle.

Fly tackle

Rods

The best fly rods are made from carbon-fibre blanks. These are very expensive. Hollow-glass fly rods are more reasonable in price and perform well under most conditions. A rod of 8 ft 6 in or 9 ft (2.6 or 2.75 m), designed to cast a no. 8 fly line, is ideal for all-round use. For all 'put and take' fisheries, two types of fly line are essential: a floating line for use when fish are feeding on or just below the surface and a sinking line for use when, as often happens, the trout are feeding close to the bottom. A double-tapered line is the best type to puchase to begin with.

Reels

Some of the low-cost fly reels available are excellent value. Remember, however, when purchasing your fly reel to make sure that the spool is large enough to hold both the fly line and at least 50 yards (45 m) of nylon or braided backing. To save money, purchase one reel plus a spare spool. One spool can be used for the floating line and the other for the sinking line.

Casts

Specially-tapered fly casts can be bought from most tackle shops. To cut costs, many anglers prefer to use a straight length of nylon from a standard spool of line. For all-round work a 50 yard (45 m) spool of 5 lb (2.3 kg) breaking-strain nylon should provide enough leader material for a season's fishing. To join the cast to the fly line I use what is known as a needle knot (see Fig. 66) to attach a short length of 15 lb (6.8 kg) breaking strain to the fly line. The cast is then knotted directly to this heavier nylon. To tie a needle knot the end of the fly line should be trimmed neatly. A sharp needle should then be inserted up through the inner core of the fly line, and at approximately $\frac{3}{8}$ or 1 in (1 or 2$\frac{1}{2}$ cm) up the line, the needle should be pushed through the outer sheath of the line. Push the needle well out and apply gentle heat from a match to the needle point. Finally withdraw the heated section of the needle from the line. This will leave a large enough hole for the heavy nylon to slide through. The needle knot shown in the Fig. 66 can then be tied, to complete the leader snood.

Flies

To begin with the angler should purchase only a few fly patterns. I suggest Ginger Quill, Iron Blue Dun and Greenwells Glory for surface work and Dog Nobbler, Muddler Minnow and Jersey Herd for bottom work. These are all good fish-catchers and can be relied upon to produce sport. Other patterns can be added to the range at a later date.

Ordinary tackle

Rods

For both worm-fishing and spinning I use an ultra light 8 ft 6 in (2.6 m) fibreglass fly rod, which I find will cast a light bait a long way and yet still have enough backbone to stop a good fish from gaining its hiding place and so breaking the tackle. When it comes to catching a really big, old cannibal trout I prefer to use something stronger such as a rod of the Avon-type.

Reels

For all-round trouble-free trout fishing of the non-fly-fishing kind, a small fixed-spool reel is the best type. With this it is possible to cast easily and accurately, which is a most necessary factor when fishing small overgrown trout waters.

(Fig. 66)

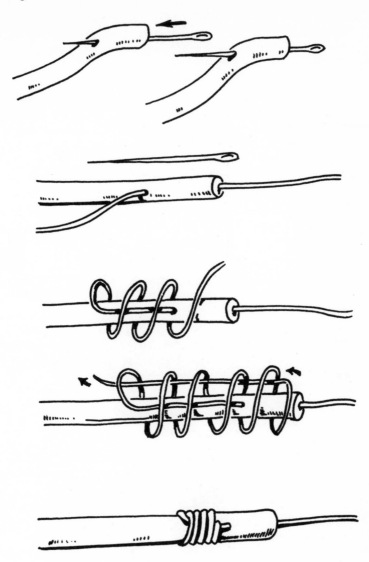

The modified needle knot (see text for details)

Lines

When worm-fishing or spinning for trout of average size, a breaking strain of 2½ lb (1.1 kg) will suffice. This light line is of no use for very large specimens, so when I set out to catch big cannibal trout I use a heavier line, 5 or 6 lb (2.3 or 2.7 kg) breaking strain at the least.

Hooks

For worm-fishing, a size 8 or 10 Model Perfect eyed hook is the most suitable. Some people, however, still prefer to use the old-fashioned Pennell tackle (see Fig. 67), but I find that the two hooks are liable to catch up on the stream bed and are more trouble than they are worth. When catching very large trout I use either a small treble or a size 4 single hook.

(Fig. 67)

Pennell tackle

Spinners

Although trout will accept most types of artificial lures, I normally use only three varieties (see Fig. 68): small fly spoons, Devon minnows and the smaller types of bar spoon.

(Fig. 68)

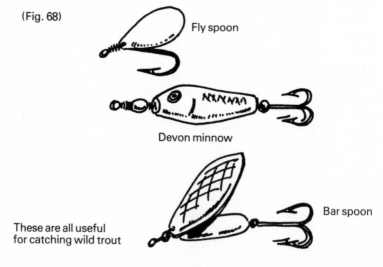

Fly spoon

Devon minnow

Bar spoon

These are all useful
for catching wild trout

Methods

Fly casting

Contrary to popular belief, fly casting is not difficult. The simplest way of explaining the basic technique is by diagrams (see Fig. 69). The six drawings explain the six movements needed to cast a fly. In position (1) the rod tip is first dropped down towards the line and the water, and, then, using the forearm and wrist, pulled rapidly upwards to position (2). Without pausing, this movement should be carried through to position (3). A brief pause is now called for. This pause allows the rod to straighten up, which automatically pulls the line out behind the caster. The weight of the line then pulls the rod tip backwards into position (4). To finish, the cast is brought forward through position (5) until it finishes up in position (6). It is essential not to start this forward movement until the line has straightened out behind you. Initially the novice caster should look back over his or her shoulder and watch the line as it floats out behind. If the forward cast is started too soon, the line will either fall in a heap just in front of the angler or the fly will be cracked off the cast with a bang. The most important part of fly casting is the timing. Once this is mastered long casts can be achieved with ease. Always remember that the longer the line you have out, the longer the pause before the rod is brought forward to position (6). To work out extra line, you must learn to 'shoot' line. This is simply a matter of false casting, pulling out extra line during the six stages of the casting process. At no time should the line be allowed to touch the water during the false casting (the idea is to work free enough line to reach a rising fish in a specific area). Finally, when sufficient line has been aerialised, the fly can be dropped on the water.

This technique sounds far more difficult than it actually is. An hour's casting practice should enable the novice fly fisherman to cast a reasonably decent amount of line.

Upstream worming

Folk lore suggests that worm-fishing for trout practically causes the fish to commit suicide, this is not true! Although I will admit that, in the hands of an expert, it can be an extremely efficient method. It is, however, a style of angling that needs a great many hours of patient practice before exceptional bags of fish

(Fig. 69)

(1) Drop the rod tip towards line and water, then

(2) pull upwards rapidly, using forearm and wrist,

(3) this will carry line through. Now pause to allow line to run back

(4) and let the weight of the line
pull back the rod. Now cast forward

(5) through this position

(6) until the line ends up thus

can be caught. The purpose of the upstream worm is to make the trout believe that the bait has simply fallen into the river and is completely unattached to hook and line. This natural movement can best be accomplished by casting the worm to the fast water at the head of a pool, and then letting the action of the current roll it over the pebbles or between the weed beds until it is either taken by a fish or can be lifted out and cast up once again to the head of the pool.

A reasonably tight line should be kept between the rod top and bait. Bites will be registered by the line tightening suddenly or by a quick pull on the rod tip. I prefer to hold a loop of line in my reel hand and feel for the pull of a taking fish. By using this method I know the exact moment a trout takes the worm and can time the strike so that the fish is hooked just inside its mouth. In this way it is simple enough to extract the hook and return the trout to the water if it is not big enough to keep. Unfortunately, no matter how quick an angler's reactions are, there are always one or two trout that swallow the baited worm. It is of little use trying to extract a hook embedded deep in the fish's throat, for invariably the fish will die. So it is more humane to knock the fish on the head, even if it is undersized; there is no point in leaving a damaged trout to die a slow death.

Although most trout will be found at the top of the pool, the tail end will often hold a good specimen. It is advisable, therefore, to try the shallows first. Otherwise, if a trout is in the area, it will flee upstream at the angler's approach, disturbing the rest of the pool as it goes.

On very small streams it is quite easy, if care is not taken, to empty the water of fish. To prevent this, it is wise to set oneself a limit, perhaps taking two to four fish only at each visit. Also, whenever possible, all trout below a certain weight or size should be returned unharmed.

Spinning

When spinning for trout the angler should present the bait in much the same way as with an upstream worm, the only difference being that as the spinner comes downstream from the deeper water the rate of retrieve must be stepped up. This keeps the lure up and away from the stream bed. Trout will often bite as the spinner enters the shallows, so it is best to be prepared at all times, striking as soon as the fish hits the bait. An extremely light lure is needed for very shallow water.

Sink-and-draw minnow

A natural minnow fished in the sink-and-draw style is an excellent lure and one which will catch trout at most times and under a wide variety of conditions. All that is needed for a complete day's fishing is half a dozen minnows, either fresh caught or preserved. Trout undoubtedly prefer a fresh bait, but it is not always possible to obtain minnows when and where they are needed.

The terminal tackle is quite simple and should be made up beforehand. It comprises a six or eight inch (15 or 20 cm) nylon trace, to which a size 10 or 12 eyed treble hook is attached. On the other end of this short trace a small loop is tied. A baiting needle is needed. These can be bought in most tackle shops and I always carry half a dozen, as it is easy to mislay one or drop it in long grass and have the day spoiled because it cannot be found.

Once again a fly rod and fixed-spool reel will be the best combination to use. Having threaded the line through the rod rings a small drilled bullet should be slipped on to the reel line, then a small link-swivel tied to the end. This will serve two purposes, first it will stop the lead from working down the trace towards the minnow and secondly, the swivel will stop most of the line kink that is common with spinning and sink-and-draw styles.

The next step is to thread the looped end of the trace through the eye of the baiting needle, then thread the trace through the dead minnow. This operation should start at the bait's vent and come out through the mouth. When this has been done, the line is pulled through the fish until the treble hook lies snugly under the bait (see Fig. 70). The needle is then removed and the loop on the trace engaged with the link on the swivel. Next, a small split shot is nipped on the line above the weight so that the lead is within about ten inches (25 cm) of the minnow at all times.

The way to use the sink-and-draw method is simple. The tackle is cast out and when the lead is felt to touch bottom a few turns of the reel make it rise. As the winding-in process stops so the movement of the minnow changes, and it flutters down in short glinting movements to the river bed. As soon as the minnow has had time to sink almost to the bottom the process is repeated until a trout intercepts the bait or a new cast is called for. I have had extremely good bags of trout with this method and have noticed that it will often take fish when all else fails.

(Fig. 70)

Minnow mounted for sink-and-draw method

Sea Trout

The sea trout is of the same species as the brown trout, the only difference being that, for some unknown reason, sea trout decide at an early age that they are not too happy with streams and river life and decide to migrate. The most interesting fact is that whereas the majority of the fish that remain behind never exceed a pound (0.45 kg) in weight, the sea trout grow into lusty fish. Where the sea trout go once they reach the open sea remains a mystery. It is known that some stay close to the river mouths, feeding on prawns and small fish, but the majority disperse.

Sea trout vary a great deal in size, but they average 2 to 3 lb (0.9–1.4 kg). However, much larger specimens have been caught; fish up to 18 lb (8.2 kg) being a possibility.

Feeding habits

Although they do not, as a rule, feed much in fresh water, a sea trout will take a fly, a small fish or the odd worm and can be easily tempted by the angler's bait, whether it be presented on the surface, at mid-water or on the bottom.

Sea trout fall readily to worms or maggots. Worms can be very effective, especially if the river happens to be in spate: at times like these, when the water runs high and coloured, sea trout move out of the main current and can often be seen leaping in the quieter waters.

Sea trout are fascinated by spinners and will often run again and again at a lure. I prefer a bar spoon, especially of the gold variety. I do not know why sea trout prefer gold to silver, but the fact remains that a golden lure attracts far more fish than any other shade.

Devon minnows also make good sea-trout lures but, unfortunately, the lures have a tendency to be rather heavy in the nose and this causes them to become snagged, especially if the bait has to be retrieved slowly as the fish are feeding well down.

Location

Sea trout can be found in all parts of the British Isles. Very big sea trout are often found in the more muddy slow-flowing rivers, such as the Sussex Ouse, which twists and turns through the flat Sussex fields.

Tackle

Rods

For spinning or bait fishing, a rod powerful enough to deal with the occasional monster yet supple enough to give sport with the smaller fish is essential. I use a glass MkIV Avon rod. The advantage of the MkIV Avon is that it is 10 ft (3 m) long which helps greatly when casting, and also when playing a fish.

Reels

I recommend a fixed-spool reel.

Lines

Where the sea trout are known to be large, it is common sense to use a line with a breaking strain of 6 or 7 lb (2.7 or 3.2 kg), but on rivers where the fish average between 1 and 3 lb (0.45–1.4 kg) a line with a 4 lb (1.8 kg) test will be required.

When bait fishing it is wise to carry a selection of eyed hooks ranging from size 6 to 16.

Methods

Legering is the best method to use when bait fishing. The whole idea being to use only the smallest amount of lead that will satisfactorily sink the worm. This ensures that the bait sinks slowly and moves from time to time as the current rolls the lead around. When fishing a known sea trout lie, it is better to use a heavier lead to keep the bait in one position.

Float

Where the water is fairly snag-free float fishing can be a most pleasant method of taking fish. Maggots seem to be the best bait for this method, probably because handfuls of the hook bait can be thrown in from time to time to encourage the fish to feed.

It is interesting to note that a bait that catches sea trout on one day will be ignored the next, and it is always necessary to experiment with baits to find out what the fish prefer. One day they may accept only ten or twelve maggots, whereas on the next day they may refuse everything except a single maggot on a size 16 hook.

Fly fishing

Sea trout respond well to the fly-fishing techniques, particularly when these methods are used at night. The fly tackle described in the Trout chapter can be used for sea-trout fishing. Sea trout show a marked preference for dark flies; a black lure being an ideal starting pattern.

Zander

A great deal of controversy has raged about the subject of zander in recent years, with some water authorities now regretting the introduction of these sleek and powerful fish. It is true that zander have rapidly extended their range in recent seasons but, at present, they seem to have balanced out after their initial population explosion.

Personally, I do not think that zander are as much of a nuisance as they are made out to be. Like all predatory species, they make inroads into the stocks of coarse fish, but nature has a way of keeping things under control and in some areas, where the rivers were overrun by tiny fish such as bleak and minnow, the zander may well have had a beneficial effect.

Location

Zander are still basically confined to the Fenland areas of East Anglia. They can also be found in the lakes at Woburn Abbey and in one or two club lakes. Rumour has it that they have been introduced illegally into other areas as well, but as yet there is little evidence of this.

Methods

Most zander are caught with basic pike-fishing techniques. Single hooks are often substituted for the treble hooks used in pike fishing and as a rule smaller baits are used. Tiny deadbaits are particularly effective for zander of all sizes. Zander can be caught on artificial baits but natural baits produce the best results.

Index

Numbers in *italic* refer to the numbered colour illustrations in the colour section.

Antenna floats 42
Audible bite indicators 40

Bait
  for barbel 10
  for bream 17
  for carp 34
    crucian carp 48
  for chub 54
  for dace 60
  for eels 68
  for grayling 74
  for perch 79
  for pike 87
  for roach 111
  for rudd 121
  for tench 126
  for trout 136, 139
    sea trout 145
  for zander 147
Bar spoons 92, 138
Barbel 9-15, *1, 2*
  bait 10
  feeding habits 10
  methods 12-15
  tackle 11-12
Bread as bait for carp 35, 44
Breadcrust as bait for rudd 122
Bream 16-32, *3, 4, 5, 6, 7*
  bait 17-19
  feeding habits 17
  handling 31-32
  location 21
  methods 28-30
  tackle 22-27
Butt-bite indicator 25, 82

Carp, 33-47, *8, 10, 12*
  bait 34
  feeding habits 34
  handling 47
  location 37
  methods 41-47
  tackle 37-40
Carp, crucian 47-52, *9, 11*
  bait 48-49
  feeding habits 48
  location 49
  methods 51
  tackle 50
Chub 53-59, *13, 15*
  bait 54
  feeding habits 53
  methods 56-59
  tackle 55-56
Combination baits for bream 18-19
Conservation 8, 31, 34

Dace 60-66, *16*
  bait 60
  feeding habits 60
  location 61
  methods 62-66
  tackle 62
Deadbaiting
  see subheading methods *under names of
    individual fish*
Devon minnow 138
Drennan feeder 30-31

Eels 67-73
  bait 68
  feeding habits 68

Eels *continued*
  location 68
  methods 71
  tackle 70

Float fishing
  for barbel 12-14
  for bream 28
  for carp 41, 51
  for chub 56
  for dace 62-63
  for grayling 75
  for perch 83-84
  for pike 93-97, 103-104
  for roach 116-117
  for rudd 123-124
  for tench 128-129
  for trout 146
Floats 42, 93, 94, 97, 116, 117, 124
Flies
  dry 57, 66, 77, 136
  wet 57, 65, 66, 77, 136
Fly fishing
  for chub 57
  for dace 64
  for grayling 77
  for rudd 124-125
  for trout 134, 139, 140-141, 146, *41,
    43, 46*
Fly line 65, 135
Flyspoon 138
Forceps 101-102

Grayling 74-77, *17, 18, 19, 20, 22, 23, 42*
  bait 74
  feeding habits 74
  methods 75
  tackle 75
Groundbait
  see subheading feeding habits *under
    names of individual fish*

Hempseed as bait for roach 113,
  117-118
Hooks 82
  see subheading tackle *under names of
    individual fish*

Jointed plugs 92

Keepnets 39

Leads
  see subheading tackle *under names of
    individual fish*

Legering
  for barbel 14
  for bream 29
  for carp 42, 51
  for chub 56
  for dace 63
  for eels 71
  for perch 84-85
  for pike 99, 105-106
  for roach 119
  for rudd 124
  for tench 130
Lines
  see subheading tackle *under names of
    individual fish*
Livebaiting
  see subheading methods *under names of
    individual fish*

Needle Knot 136-137

Orfe *14*

Pennell tackle 138
Perch 78-86, *21, 24, 25*
  baits 79
  feeding habits 79
  location 80
  methods 83
  tackle 81-83
Pike 87-108, *26, 27, 28, 29, 30, 31, 32*
  bait 88-89, *29*
  feeding habits 88
  location 89
  methods 93
  tackle 90-93
Plug bait *29*
Potato as bait for carp 36

Reels
  see subheading tackle *under names of
    individual fish*
Roach 109-119, *33, 34, 35*
  bait 111
  feeding habits 111
  location 114
  methods 116
  tackle 114-116
Rods
  see subheading tackle *under names of
    individual fish*
Rudd 120-125, *36, 37*
  bait 121-132
  feeding habits 120-121
  methods 123-125
  tackle 123

Sausage as bait for barbel 11
Spinning
    for chub 57
    for perch 80
    for pike 92-93, 106-108
    for trout 142-144
Sweetcorn 19, 36
Swing tip and target 23-25

Tench 126-133, *38*, *39*, *40*, *42*
    baits 126-127
    feeding habits 126
    location 127
    methods 128-133
    tackle 127-128
Traces
    see subheading tackle *under names of*
        individual fish

Trout 134-144, *19*, *41*, *43*, *44*, *45*, *46*,
    47, *48*
    feeding habits 135
    location 135
    methods 139
    tackle 135-138
Trout, sea 144-146
    baits 146
    feeding habits 144
    methods 146
    tackle 145-146

Wobbling spoon 92
Wobbling tackle 108

Zander 147, *49*
    location 147
    methods 147